W9-BZR-251

The Official

NANCY DREW®

Handbook

SKILLS, TIPS & LIFE LESSONS FROM EVERYONE'S FAVORITE GIRL DETECTIVE

PENNY WARNER

QUIRK BOOKS
PHILADELPHIA

Published by Quirk Productions, Inc.

Library of Congress Cataloging in Publication Number: 2007927223

ISBN: 978-1-59474-194-4

Printed in China

Typeset in Legacy

Designed by Bryn Ashburn
Illustrations by Jesse Ewing
Edited by Mindy Brown
Production management by Chris Veneziale

Distributed in North America by Chronicle Books
680 Second Street
San Francisco, CA 94107

10 9 8 7 6 5 4 3 2 1

Quirk Books
215 Church Street
Philadelphia, PA 19106
www.quirkbooks.com

For mystery-solving tips, a sleuthing blog, and more Nancy e-fun, visit

NANCYDREWFOREVER.COM

Warning!

Not everyone has the innate talent and incredible luck that Nancy Drew possesses. Please use caution when attempting any of the tips or skills described in this handbook. As much as we've made every effort to provide for accuracy of information and your personal safety, if this books falls into the wrong hands, the outcome cannot be guaranteed. Much like a Nancy Drew mystery, this book is designed for entertainment purposes and should be used only at your own risk (see "How to Gain the Courage to Take Risks," page 13). The information contained within these pages is a general guide and not a replacement for taking classes from professionals in the areas that interest you. If you want to become an expert like Nancy, enroll in a course, study the subject for years, practice for hours, and make sure you have medical coverage and insurance in case of a mishap. We—the authors, publishers, and experts—disclaim any liability from any harm, injury, damage, litigation, weight gain, broken nails, bad hair, or anything else that might occur as a result of owning, reading, or following anything in this handbook. Remember, Nancy would never break the law, put anyone in jeopardy, or do anything foolhardy, even to solve a mystery, and we recommend that you follow her example. That said, set your jaw, keep your wits about you, have a cup of tea handy, and if you find yourself in danger, be sure to yell, "Help!"

Contents

Introduction

Welcome, super sleuths, girl gumshoes, and detectives in training.

Somehow, through brilliant detecting, deduction of clues, or simply following a hunch, you've found *The Official Nancy Drew® Handbook*. Within these bound covers you'll discover Nancy's most closely guarded secrets of sleuthing, gathered through years of gifted detective work.

No doubt you've always wondered how to trail criminals in your blue roadster without mussing your hair, investigate haunted houses after escaping rope bonds, send top-secret messages to your loyal sidekicks using only red lipstick and high-heeled shoes, and uncover lost wills concealed within hidden passageways. But if you follow in Nancy's footsteps, you're almost guaranteed success in *all* areas of your life, from choosing your faithful friends to being happy even when your life is full of criminals, crooks, and creeps.

In the pages that follow, you'll learn how to tell if a man is attracted to you, how to flirt (and garner clues), how to tell the bad guys from the good guys—and even how to keep romance alive, as Nancy and Ned have managed to do for decades. You'll also learn how to use beauty products for sleuthing and remain poised when the situation is dire—as well as how to pack the perfect handbag for all detecting contingencies.

You'll discover the girl sleuth's essential pointers on how to gather clues to solve a mystery, how to tell if someone is lying, how to follow a suspect (or two-timing boyfriend), and how to locate a secret passageway—not to mention how to train a carrier pigeon to send important messages to your chums.

Nancy, of course, also knows a thing or two about survival. After all, she's miraculously managed to escape all sorts of harrowing situations. Here you'll learn how to escape from quicksand or a locked car trunk, fend off a poisonous snake or hungry alligator, avoid being hypnotized or drugged, and extricate your car from a ditch.

Nancy is skilled at just about everything she does, and you can be, too. This step-by-step how-to guide contains essential advice on how to tame a wild bucking horse, analyze suspicious handwriting, and maneuver a sabotaged canoe. It also provides a collection of Nancy's first-aid essentials to treat everything from fainting spells to snakebites to swollen limbs.

These secrets and many others have never before been revealed, so guard this insider's guide closely. Many nefarious characters with broken noses, crinkly ears, square jaws, and shifty eyes would happily kidnap, chloroform, strike, or suffocate you to get their hands on this valuable information.

So grab your flashlight and your chums, head for that hidden attic, haunted bridge, or moss-covered mansion, and start sleuthing. There is no mystery too baffling to solve. After all, you've got Nancy in your handbag—and she's got your back.

CHAPTER 1

Clues to Success in Relationships & Life

Set a Goal and Stick to It

"I'm going to keep working on this case until all the pieces in the puzzle can be made to fit together!" Nancy told her father.
—The Ghost of Blackwood Hall

When Nancy sets her mind to something, nothing gets in her way, even when she doubts her own ability to succeed. Nancy knew at a young age she wanted to be a detective and help her father with his legal cases. Over the years she's proved herself a crackerjack sleuth, mainly because she never gives up. Here are steps to setting—and meeting—your own goals.

1 Brainstorm.

Nancy has set a wide variety of goals, everything from learning tennis, piano, and horseback riding to helping at the crippled children's home to becoming a super sleuth. Think about all the things you'd like to accomplish or achieve. Include even your wildest dreams, in all areas of your life, such as education, career, relationships, physical skills, financial status, and service to the community.

2 Focus on realistic goals.

Even Nancy knows she can't do everything, so she focuses on realistic goals. Take a close look at your list and decide which goals you want to pursue the most. Make sure they're realistic and play to your strengths rather than your weaknesses. Be honest about why you want to achieve them. Set positive goals rather than negative ones. For example, don't state the goal as "I'll stop being afraid." Instead write, "I'll try to be braver."

3 *Separate short-term goals from long-term ones.*

Nancy's long-term goal is to be the best detective she can be. Her short-term goals focus on solving mysteries, one clue at a time. Divide your goals into two categories: short-term (those you can reach in a few days, weeks, or months) and long-term (those that may take years or a lifetime). Next, prioritize the goals, setting them in order of importance.

4 *Break the goals into steps.*

Do some careful planning for your goals. Create a time-line for each of the steps. List tasks to accomplish each day, each week, and each month to keep you headed toward your goal. Check off each task as you complete it.

5 *Recheck your goals and steps periodically.*

Your goals may change over time, or you may find that the steps you've outlined are not realistic and need to be revised. Don't obsess about setbacks or incomplete tasks. Move on after you alter the steps to your goals.

6 *Stay focused.*

Nancy constantly reviews her sleuthing to-do list, and at the end of each successful case, she gives herself a reward to remind her of her hard work and perseverance. Review your goals each day. Look at what you've accomplished so far and reward yourself for those achievements. Build on these successes to help you keep going.

7 Reevaluate failures.

If you have trouble meeting a goal, there may be an underlying reason. See if you can analyze the problem and either overcome the block or let it go. It may be an unattainable goal. Make sure the goal is what you want, not what others want for you. Don't forget—you learn from your setbacks, too.

Consider all the goals you'd like to accomplish or achieve.

Gain the Courage to Take Risks

Nancy always shows great courage in dangerous situations, whether it's chasing after criminals, climbing rafters to escape, or scaling castle walls, commando-style, to investigate a clue. Although she admits her fears, she doesn't let them overwhelm her. Courage to take risks comes in many forms, from saving a kidnap victim to exploring a hidden passageway to exposing a ghost. Here are steps to facing—and overcoming—the fears that stand in your way.

1 *Figure out why you're hesitant to take a risk.*

When most people are confronted with a risk, they think about the consequences. This keeps them from doing foolish things, like picking up a stranger along the road or walking into an obvious trap. But this hesitation can turn into a general fear that may be debilitating and keep you from experiencing new adventures. The key is to find a balance between risk and consequence.

2 *Demystify the risk.*

For Nancy, taking a risk is more about having a positive attitude and less about the negative label. She goes right to the core of the task quickly to find out whether or not it's a safe thing to do. For you, this may mean moving out of your comfort zone—a frightening thought for many. Instead of calling it a risk, change your negative attitude and think of it as a positive adventure, a journey, an exploration, a learning experience, or the next step in your overall development.

3 Look at the situation realistically.

Instead of seeing a risk as a black-and-white, do-or-die situation, recognize the gray areas and degrees of success. Keep your eye on the big picture—the results of taking the risk—and don't get bogged down in the details that prevent you from achieving your goal.

4 Examine the consequences honestly.

Think about what you have to lose when you take the risk and what you may gain. Will you be able to handle the consequences?

5 Focus on the desired outcome.

Nancy never loses sight of her goal. List everything that you'll gain from taking the risk. Think about how it will affect other areas of your life and how you will build on it. See this as taking one step leading to another, and so on. Remember, you have the freedom to choose—taking the risk is your decision to make.

6 Start small and work your way up.

If something is holding you back, there may be a reason. Break the challenge into smaller steps and try to take that first step toward your goal. It doesn't have to be all or nothing in the beginning.

7 Begin today.

One of the best ways to overcome those fears and gain courage is to take action now. There is no better time than today.

8 Learn from your failures.

Even Nancy has a failure now and then, but it stops her only temporarily. Just because you failed at taking a particular risk, that doesn't mean you'll fail at everything. Evaluate the situation, see if you could have done something differently, and make changes next time.

9 Look for signs that indicate a bad risk.

Don't take a risk if:
- You could lose something important—or everything.
- You can't fix the outcome if it goes wrong.
- There are essential factors you can't control.
- You sense the outcome is not worth the risk.

Choose Your Faithful Sidekicks

Bess, blond and pretty, had a penchant for second desserts and frilly dresses. She shared Nancy's adventures out of a deep loyalty to her but was constantly fearful of the dangers involved. George was as boyish as her name. Her hair was dark, her face handsomely pert. George wore simple clothes and craved adventure. —The Secret of the Wooden Lady

Nancy has lots of friends, from Helen Corning to Ned Nickerson, and from Hannah Gruen to her father, Carson Drew. But it's her two faithful sidekicks—Bess, pretty, slightly plump, blonde; and George, slender, athletic, boyish—who became her lifelong sleuthing pals. Here are steps to help you find your own loyal, dependable sidekicks.

1 Decide what kind of sidekick you want.

Nancy likes Bess and George because they offer different strengths. Think about who you want by your side in case of danger or an emergency. Do you want:

- A sidekick who shares similar traits with you?
- A sidekick who offers different traits to complement yours?
- A quiet sidekick who doesn't get on your nerves?
- A lively sidekick who offers ideas and suggestions?
- A male sidekick who can handle heavy tasks or dirty jobs?
- A female sidekick who will understand your moods and share clothes?

2 *Make sure your choice has all the hallmark sidekick traits.*

Bess and George have all the traits required for a sidekick, including trustworthiness, loyalty, honesty, a keen sense of justice, and eagerness to help.

3 *Treat your sidekick well.*

Your sidekick will be there for you if you treat her with respect, give her praise when deserved, and help her in her time of need.

4 *Give your sidekick important tasks.*

Most sidekicks would rather be the heroes, but they're willing to remain in the secondary role if they feel they're also doing important work. Give your sidekick specific jobs to assist you in your tasks, then let her know how pleased you are at her successes.

5 *Protect your sidekick in dangerous situations.*

A sidekick is not usually as strong and confident as you, so she may need protection when things become difficult or dangerous. Bess is often fearful when it comes to detecting, and George is sometimes overly confident. Watch your sidekick's back, make sure she's safe, and do what you can to rescue her if she's in jeopardy.

6 *Remember to take breaks.*

Don't forget that sidekicks need a break now and then. Plan a day of picnicking, a canoe trip with the guys, a game of shuffleboard, or other activity for a fun time. A teatime break is always appreciated in times of stress.

7 *Compromise when disagreements arise.*

Your sidekick may not always agree with your decisions and may challenge you. Even Bess and George sometimes question Nancy's plans. Explain your reasoning, and try to understand her side of the argument. Apologize if you're in the wrong, and make an effort to find a happy medium so you both can feel comfortable with the decision.

8 *Accept her for who she is.*

You can't change your sidekick's personality or temperament, so learn to accept her the way she is. If a sidekick is fearful, like Bess, allow her to stand back and watch rather than participate. If a sidekick is quick to get angry, like George, try to calm her down and give her something constructive to do to help dissipate her ire. If a sidekick has an annoying habit, such as yelling "Hypers!" when in distress, try to appreciate this as an endearing quirk.

Negotiate with Difficult People

Nancy must deal with difficult people every day—criminals, crooks, cowards, people of questionable ethics—yet she maintains her poise, rarely flies off the handle, and always makes the best of situations. Difficult people can be a challenge, but there are ways to help you cope.

1 Determine the type of difficult person.

- **Aggressive**—Essentially a bully, like Nathan Gomber from *The Hidden Staircase*, he will try to intimidate you. Stand up to him, be assertive without being aggressive, and don't overreact. Eventually he will run out of steam.

- **Passive-aggressive**—Like that sneaky Jemitt in *The Mystery of the Twisted Candles*, he takes potshots at others and makes sneak attacks. The best way to deal with him is direct confrontation.

- **Complainer**—Like Mrs. Allison from *The Mystery of the Ivory Charm*, this person doesn't feel she can effect change, so she complains instead. Maintan a positive attitude to counter her complaints.

- **Silent**—Much like Grizzle Face in *The Mystery of the Brass-Bound Trunk*, he may not respond at all or offer only short, snappy answers to questions. Ask him questions that require more than a yes/no response, then wait patiently for an answer.

2 *Don't take the behavior personally.*

Rude characters, villains, thugs, scoundrels, and rogues all behave the way they do for reasons unrelated to you—unless you happen to be snooping into their criminal activities.

3 *Don't try to change a difficult person.*

You can't control a person like Stumpy Dowd, Foxy Felix, or Zany Shaw, so instead of trying to alter his actions and words, change the way you respond to him.

4 *Make sure the problem isn't yours.*

Examine your feelings to make sure you're not overreacting. Share your feelings with a friend to see if she recognizes the problem, too. If the problem is yours, deal with it.

5 *Brainstorm ways to cope.*

Jot down the various ways you can deal with the difficult person, such as ignoring him, confronting him, having him removed from the situation, or perhaps investigating him to see if there's something behind the behavior.

6 *Confront the person calmly.*

Share your feelings and concerns, using "I" messages, such as "I don't like that you've been tailing me" or "I'd prefer you didn't try to overhear my conversations."

7 *Try to reach a compromise.*

Agree to be pleasant to one another—or avoid one another as a last resort.

Supervise Others

Nancy is a take-charge kind of girl, whether she's watching over a runaway child, directing her sleuthing chums, asking for help from her housekeeper, or ordering criminals around. If you're timid about supervising others, take some tips from Nancy's style of command.

1 Decide what kind of assistance you need.

When Nancy is on a case, she defines the problem before determining what type of assistance she needs. If it's household chores, she may need her trusted housekeeper. If it's solving a mystery, she engages her chums for help. If she's dealing with a criminal, she knows it's best to call in professional help from the local police.

2 Don't order. Ask.

Nancy uses tact when she wants something done. She never makes commands, which may cause the other person to be defensive. Nancy is always polite when she asks, and therefore she finds people eager to assist with her investigations.

3 Explain the task in detail.

Define the job as specifically as you can so the person knows what her responsibilities are. For example, when Nancy is on a stakeout, she assigns specific jobs to Bess and George or Ned. Ask questions to make sure your requests are understood, and see if your assistants have any questions. Clarify your goals, set deadlines, and then show your team that you have confidence in their work.

4 Encourage independence.

It's not easy to supervise others all the time. If you are working with a team, encourage them to work independently, yet still under your direction. Make sure each is a good fit for the task. For example, Bess is better at guarding the car during an investigation, while George is better at taking action. Check on your assistants from time to time to offer suggestions or see if they need any help from you.

5 Praise their accomplishments.

Let your team know that their work is appreciated. Recognize their achievements and reward them with praise or a gift. They'll show their appreciation by continuing to help you on future cases.

HOW TO

Remain Poised in Dire Situations

Even Nancy Drew loses her cool once in a while, but she tries not to show it. When her heart is in her throat or her brow is knit in worry, she remains positive and focused until the problem is solved and the danger is abated.

1 Have a worry session.

If you must worry, then take a few minutes to really focus on the problem. Write down your concerns, then tell yourself that the worry session is over and move on.

2 Clear your mind.

Take a break, take a nap, or take a run to dissolve the clutter from your mind. Close your eyes, think of something peaceful, and focus on deep breathing.

3 Don't try to control the world.

When you realize that you cannot control everything and everyone, you'll begin to accept the things you can change and work on them. Let go of the rest, and the stress will disappear.

4 Try affirmations.

When the situation is tense, pause, take a few deep breaths, and repeat an affirmation, such as "Calm down" or "Strong, capable girls always succeed when the going gets tough."

5 Avoid dangerous or upsetting situations.

Nancy knows when it's not safe to enter a questionable situation by herself. She waits until she's sure there's no danger, or she brings along help. If your upsetting situation can't be avoided, however, then at least be prepared. (See page 28.)

6 Think before you act.

When you're faced with a stressful problem, take a few minutes to consider all your options. Move forward only when you're aware of all possibilities and outcomes.

7 Change habits that lead to tension.

Think about what habits are contributing to your stress and try to change them. For example, switch from coffee to herbal tea, cut down on sugar and desserts, replace sodas with bottled water, and avoid going into creepy cabins or abandoned warehouses.

8 Seek professional help.

If you continue to experience stress and have disturbing thoughts in spite of your efforts, consider getting professional help.

Savor the Important Things in Life, Like a Rich Cup of Hot Cocoa

Nancy is happy because she's competent, confident, and in control. She loves what she does, she cares about her friends and family, and she knows how to savor the important things in life, like a rich cup of hot cocoa or walk through nature. She also has a sense of humor, which keeps her from being overwhelmed by the many problems associated with solving mysteries, such as being covered in mud or mussing her hair. If you need some tips on how to be happy, try the following:

1 *Have something hot.*

When Nancy has a mystery on her mind and is stuck, she has a hot bowl of soup, cup of tea, or mug of cocoa. Or she hops into a warm bath to soothe her and recharge her batteries. By the time she's finished, her spirits are lifted considerably.

2 *Take in nature.*

Nancy often takes a walk outside to breathe in the morning air, explore the rose garden, and let the beauty of nature sink in. Get some air and clear your brain, so that afterward you can think further about your knotty problems.

3 *Keep your cool.*

Even in the most desperate situations, Nancy repeatedly tells herself to stay calm. She knows that losing her confidence could be disastrous to her safety.

4 *Help others.*

Nothing makes you feel better than helping others. Nancy always makes time to work for the crippled children's home by putting on a show or doing other volunteer work, especially for kids.

5 *Start fresh tomorrow.*

When you feel everything is hopeless, get a good night's sleep and try again the next day. The situation will look better after you're rested and refreshed.

6 *Talk with friends.*

When Nancy is puzzled about a particular problem, she talks it over with her chums, her father, or her understanding housekeeper, Hannah Gruen. They offer her a new perspective on her problem, which helps her come to a solution.

7 *Share your success.*

Nancy always thanks her chums when she solves a case, claiming she couldn't have done it without them. Although that's probably not true, she prefers to share credit with others.

CHAPTER **2**

Clues to
Fashion & Beauty

HOW TO

Pack the Perfect Handbag
for All Contingencies

A good detective—and successful woman—doesn't go anywhere without a well-packed handbag, purse, or backpack. Take some tips from Nancy: You can never be too prepared when it comes to combining your active social life with the life of a girl detective.

1 Get a roomy, well-made handbag.

If you can't afford the latest bag by Louis Vuitton or Prada, shop at a mid-priced store, find a knock-off, or check the thrift store for a slightly used designer bag. Try on a number of colors and styles, making sure the bag matches most of your wardrobe. The bag should be roomy, with plenty of secret compartments to hide notes, jewels, and the like.

2 Fill it with essentials for motoring or traveling.

Include your wallet, identification, valid driver's license, passport, some cash and credit cards, your keys, emergency information, medical card, and road-side service card.

3 Include items for cosmetic maintenance.

Buy a smaller purse for your lip balm, comb or brush, lotion, hand sanitizer, nail file, makeup, handkerchief or tissues, mending kit, gum or breath mints, and mirror.

④ *Add communication devices and essential supplies.*

Pack several ballpoint pens, a pad of sticky notes, a notebook, a cell phone, business cards, and your appointment book, PDA, or address book.

⑤ *Don't forget your detecting tools.*

You never know when you'll need to solve a crime, so be sure to pack the following:

• Flashlight, with new batteries, and a backup flashlight or candle for when you're in a dark passageway.

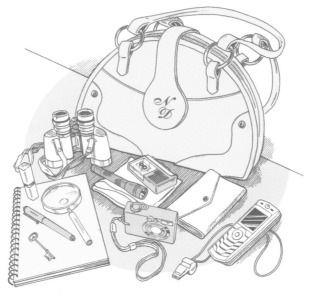

The perfect handbag is large enough
to hold all the sleuthing essentials.

- Magnifying glass, so you can read fine print, examine fingerprints, and look for details at a crime scene.
- Whistle, so you can attract the attention of your rescuers or signal each other.
- Binoculars to help you spy on suspects from a distance.
- Cell phone to alert your team or the police.
- Secret compartment, so you can hide notes, jewels, or other important clues.
- Camera to take pictures of suspects, crime scenes, and footprints. If you have a camera cell phone, that's one less thing to carry.
- Tape recorder, video camera, or other device for interviewing or surveilling suspects.
- Change of clothes, in case you fall into a muddy ravine or are spotted while tailing a suspect. Be sure to include a light jacket, preferably a reversible one, and a hat for sun protection or to hide your face.
- Map of the area you're investigating.
- Notebook and pen or pencil.
- Bail money, in case you're arrested for suspicious behavior and your father is not around to vouch for you.
- Optional: Walkie-talkies, night-vision goggles, long-distance listening devices, hidden cameras, and camouflage outfits.

6 If you still have room . . .

Try to squeeze in a paperback to read during stakeouts, some snacks, a small hatchet, a skeleton key, and a foreign-language translator.

Foiling a Purse Snatcher

At the same moment Nancy realized that her arm felt strangely light. "My handbag!" Nancy gasped. "It's gone!"—*Password to Larkspur Lane*

You can make yourself a less attractive target for purse snatchers by following these guidelines, based on the recommendations of the FBI and the National Crime Prevention Council.

- *Carry valuables in your pockets rather than in a purse. It's harder for purse snatchers to grab your money and valuables if you have them tucked into a pocket instead of dangling in a purse on your arm.*
- *Be alert at all times, and look like it. Stay aware and watch out for criminal types, such as men with long scars and crinkly ears. Keep your bag close to your body, with your hand over the clasp, and glance around frequently to discourage would-be snatchers. Use drive-up or in-store ATMs during the day, have your card ready, and check around for suspicious-looking snatchers.*
- *Keep your purse with you at all times. Don't leave it unattended in a shopping cart, on a restaurant table, or in your car, where it will tempt a potential purse snatcher.*
- *Do not display the contents of your purse. Don't expose your valuables, money, and jewels, which will attract the attention of a thief. Be discreet when paying for something, and don't flash your wad of cash.*
- *If a thief does try to snatch your purse . . . Do not attempt to fight the purse snatcher and risk injury. First yell, "Stop! Thief!" in a loud voice and point in the direction of the suspect's escape. Note the thief's characteristics—race, height, hair color, and clothing— then report these details to the police.*

Use Beauty Products to Your Best Advantage

Nancy doesn't apply a lot of makeup. What she does use, she keeps subtle—a little lipstick, some light powder, and a touch of rouge or blush. Occasionally her cosmetics come in handy for solving crimes and getting her out of desperate situations. Here are some dual appearance-enhancing and sleuthing uses for your essential beauty products.

Lipstick

Lipstick can draw seductive attention to your mouth—and it can also be substituted for blush or rouge in emergencies. Use a lip liner first, but smudge it so you don't get that "liner" look. To keep lipstick off your teeth, apply lipstick, then pop your finger into your mouth, press down, and remove your finger, along with the excess color.

For sleuthing:

- Lipstick can be used to write SOS or other words when you're in danger (see page 120).
- To avoid leaving behind evidence, keep lipstick off a drinking glass by discreetly licking the glass first.
- An empty lipstick tube makes a great place to hide jewels and coded messages.
- If you need to appear wounded, red lipstick makes an excellent stand-in for dried blood.

Eye Makeup

Hypnotize him with "smoky" eyes by applying dark eye shadow on the lids. Then line the eyes in black, brown, or gray above the upper lash, thicker in the middle. Violet, blue, and deep green liners also make beautiful smoky eyes. Use a Q-tip to blend and soften the color. Curl your lashes, then finish with volumizing mascara, both top and bottom. Use blue or purple mascara to make your eyes "pop." Try a lash comb to separate clumps, and apply the mascara in a zigzag movement.

For sleuthing:
- Mascara brushes make good weapons for stabbing a criminal or gouging his eyes.
- In an emergency, you can write a message with the tip of the mascara if you don't have a pen, pencil, or lipstick.
- Use the tube to store bits of important information.

Eyebrow Pencil and Tweezers

Get your brows professionally shaped to make your eyes appear larger. Use this shape as a blueprint for future shaping when you tweeze on your own. (You can use your magnifying glass when you tweeze.) With an eyebrow pencil, draw your eyebrow in a slight arch, a little longer than your natural brow line. If brows are sparse, fill in with more pencil or use a little brown eye shadow. Keep your brows in place by applying a dab of clear gel or lip balm.

For sleuthing:
- Use an eyebrow pencil to write emergency messages if you don't have a pen, mascara tip, or lipstick.
- Carry tweezers to pick locks, scratch out a message, or

stab a bad guy. They're also good for handling objects that may contain suspicious fingerprints.

Blush and Powder

Rouge, or blush, adds a healthy glow to any skin type. To apply, smile to find the apple of your cheeks, then brush directly on that spot. For a sexy look, add a little shimmer blush. Dusky pink will warm up skin that looks pale or tired from sleuthing.

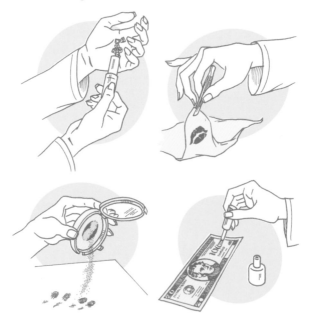

Clockwise from top left: Lipstick case for hidden jewels; tweezers for handling evidence; nail polish for marking counterfeit bills; powder for revealing fingerprints.

For sleuthing:

- Use powder or blush to retrieve fingerprints. Lightly sprinkle powder on the prints, apply a piece of clear tape, then lift off carefully to transfer the prints onto the tape.
- After closing and locking the door to your room, sprinkle powder on the floor in front of the door so that you will be able to determine whether someone has attempted to enter your room while you were out.

Nail Polish

If you don't have time for regular manicures and pedicures, just keep your nails clean and the same length. Choose a clear or light shade for everyday sleuthing, and a dark, dramatic color for evening and parties. Avoid bizarre or neon colors; you don't want to attract the wrong kind of attention, especially when you're investigating a crime.

For sleuthing:

- Use a dot of nail polish to mark bills you suspect may be counterfeit.
- If you're caught in a downpour while studying a clue bearing an important message, cover the writing with clear nail polish to preserve it.

Look Your Best When the Going Gets Tough

After an agonizing wait, Nancy poured some water from the Thermos onto her clean handkerchief and wiped her face and hands. Then she combed her hair and put on fresh lipstick. Bess giggled. "I don't know why we bother. There's no one out here to see us but prairie dogs and lizards!"—The Secret at Shadow Ranch

Whether she's sleuthing, dating, lunching with friends, or stuck out on the prairie, Nancy always knows how to keep her cool and look her best. Her favorite fashions include shapely sheaths, flowered frocks, simple suits, and elegant gowns. And a handkerchief always comes in handy. Spruce up your look with some hints from Nancy's basic wardrobe, and you'll be ready for any situation or occasion.

1 Invest in a trench coat.

A trench coat is a sleuthing necessity and a classic piece that will dress up your attire on a cold day or cover a torn or soiled outfit. It can even be worn as a belted dress in emergencies.

2 Add a little black dress.

When you want to be unobtrusive, choose a comfortable black dress that's not too binding so you have freedom of movement while maintaining some style and shape. Dress it up or down with the right accessories and you'll be able to wear it to any event, from a night at the theater to lunch at an inn to a stakeout at an abandoned warehouse.

3 Include a short-sleeved cotton T-shirt.

Sometimes sleuthing calls for casual wear, especially if you're investigating a mystery at a sporting event, quaint village, or campground. Choose a plain T-shirt that you can layer in cool weather, tie at the midriff in warm weather, or pair with patterned pants or printed skirts.

4 Buy a basic pair of slacks.

When your investigation calls for dressy pants, it's best to go with classic fitted slacks rather than the latest trend. Select a fabric that doesn't wrinkle, collect lint, or chafe. Then dress it up or down with a silky blouse or simple top for a quick change as needed.

5 Remember your old pair of jeans.

Whether you're sleuthing on a haunted bridge, retrieving a scared cat from the rafters, or exploring a dark cave, a good pair of worn, comfortable jeans will give you the opportunity to move freely, without worrying about ruining your outfit.

6 Step into a pair of sturdy pumps.

Make sure they're comfy, well constructed, and easy to slip into and out of in an emergency. Practice running in your pumps to ensure they don't fly off when you're chasing a suspect.

7 *Don't forget the all-purpose suit.*

You'll want to look professional when discussing a case with the local authorities, interviewing for an undercover job, or giving a speech on crime fighting. Buy a tailored suit in a neutral tone and accessorize it to match the situation, pairing it with a designer scarf, pretty pin, or silky blouse.

8 *Finish with a little touch of flair.*

Personalize your own basic wardrobe with that special touch—a pair of white gloves, a cloche hat, a unique necklace, or a funky belt. You might even add a corsage with a hidden microphone or designer scarf that doubles as a signal transmitter. Fashion, like sleuthing, is all about the details.

Accessorize with Flair

Nancy keeps to the basics by sporting simple frocks and matching shoes, but she adds flair with the perfect fashion accessories, such as an ivory charm necklace or gold handbag for special occasions. You can take your outfit from frumpy to fashionable if you follow a few simple clues from Nancy's closet.

1 *Keep it simple, and stay away from fads.*

Stick with two to three colors at a time. You don't want to be all one color and disappear—unless you're going undercover. But you also don't want to stick out like a bad bridesmaid's dress. Less is more, so keep it simple. Faddish clothes usually call attention to the outfit, not the person. Choose clothing that's unique, rather than opting for trendy togs popular with everyone.

2 *Add a handbag.*

Sometimes you can change the whole look of your outfit by adding an oversized bag, colorful satchel, funky pocketbook, or designer purse. Just make sure it's large enough to hold your cosmetics, sleuthing tools, and any disguises you might need. (See "How to Pack the Perfect Handbag for All Contingencies," page 28.)

3 *Include other embellishments.*

Now it's time to add a flirty hat, elegant jewelry, or a provocative scarf. Just don't go overboard. Use an embellishment that calls attention to one of your best features, not your worst. And add only one at a time.

4 *Choose your signature piece.*

Be creative with a unique signature piece that says, "This is me!" It could be a whimsical brooch, a personalized charm bracelet, an heirloom necklace, colorful socks, or a pair of flip-flops to go with every occasion. Think of ways to keep it fresh, not predictable. And don't let it draw attention away from your outfit.

Handle Fashion and Beauty Emergencies

Even the most capable girl detective has a fashion mishap now and then. But Nancy doesn't let it take over her mood or her look. With a little creativity and ingenuity, you can turn any potential disaster into a mere mild annoyance.

- **Remove makeup stains.** If you happen to get makeup stains on your undercover disguise or sleuthing suit, don't stress. Just find someone with a baby and ask if you can borrow a baby wipe. Then rub the wipe on the spot and watch it fade away. You can also use baby wipes to remove lint from your dark clothing, clean dirt from your high heels and pumps, or remove deodorant marks.

- **Fix a fallen hem.** If you're running after a suspect and accidentally catch your heel in the hem of your long skirt, you can repair it easily. Ask someone nearby—a handsome construction worker or handyman—for masking or duct tape. Then use small strips to secure the fallen fabric.

- **Keep bra straps from sliding.** When you're in the middle of an important investigation, there's nothing more irritating than having to yank up a sliding bra strap. Use double-sided tape, or even a strip of duct tape, to secure the strap to your skin.

- **Repair a broken heel.** When chasing suspects or saving

herself from harm, Nancy often accidentally breaks the heel off one of her pumps. Keep a small container of permanent glue in your handbag to repair a broken heel, reattach a loose embellishment, or fix an undone sole.

- **Unstick a zipper.** It never fails: Just when you're about to meet your prime suspect, your zipper gets stuck! Rub a bar of soap or some candle wax onto the zipper to help it slide again. If that doesn't work, use your nail scissors to cut a small slit in the zipper tape, then work the zipper around it. If the zipper breaks completely, leaving a gaping hole, ask to borrow a gentleman's sweater or girlfriend's shawl.

- **Keep from losing a loose button.** Dab the center of the button with a little clear nail polish or glue to keep the threads from breaking. If the button pops off anyway, use a metal bread tie to secure it in place.

- **Keep your sweater from unraveling.** While sleuthing in rough terrain, you're likely to catch a sweater on a rough rock or jagged edge. Back up to release the snag; do not pull it or you may find yourself with a pile of yarn. Take the tip of a closed pen or your tweezers and push the snag back through to the inside of the sweater. Knot it and secure it with a dab of clear nail polish.

- **Smooth a smudged nail.** When you lead an active life, it's hard to wait for the polish to dry. If your manicure smudges, put a drop of nail polish remover on your finger and smooth out the smudge. Then apply a light coat of polish over the whole nail.

- **Stop a shaving mishap.** If you cut yourself while shaving your legs, moisten a dry tea bag with cold water and place it on the cut to stop the bleeding.

Manage Your Hair When the Convertible Top Is Down

A little wind in her hair never slows Nancy down. She prefers to drive her convertible roadster with the top down. But if you have the kind of coiffure that doesn't hold up well after a spin in your cabriolet, here are some ways to manage those flyaway wisps and curls.

- **Use product.** Apply a styling gel to provide texture, flexibility, and shine. Or try a mousse that gives you extra hold and the ability to restyle. Look for a hair product that includes sunscreen to prevent sun damage to your precious tresses. There are even special in-the-wind hair products that prevent tangles while guarding your locks against wind damage, dirt, and dust. Top off your coif with a convertible-proof hairspray for good measure.

- **Put your hair in a ponytail or spray.** It's so easy to tie up your hair in a swinging ponytail or twist it into a carefree spray or casual chignon. Keep stretchy hair bands and colorful scrunchies in the car to use when the top is down. When you arrive at your destination, remove the bands and shake out your hair.

- **Go for the wind-blown look.** Instead of trying to tame your locks, keep your hair on the natural side, and free those curls, waves, or ringlets. Shake out your current do, then flip your head over and spray your hair liberally with hairspray. Next, flip your hair back up and style it or scrunch it with your fingers. Don't be afraid to go wild.

- **Wear a colorful scarf.** Wrap your hair in a brightly colored silk headscarf and give yourself a stylish look while keeping your hair under control. Choose a thin scarf that isn't too bulky and try for various looks:

  - Schoolgirl style—Fold the scarf into a rectangle and tie it at the nape of your neck to make a headband.
  - Gypsy style—Fold it into a triangle over your hair and tie it at the nape of your neck.
  - Babushka style—Fold it into a triangle over your hair and tie it under your chin.
  - Isadora Duncan style—Tie a long white scarf around your head and let it blow in the wind as you drive your roadster. (Caution: Do not tie it around your neck.)
- **Cut it short.** If you love having the top down and don't have time to fool with your hair, consider getting a short, spunky haircut, like George's. It's easy to care for, always looks sleek and stylish, and doesn't require any special attention while riding in the wind.

Cope with a Bad Hair Day and Other Hair Emergencies

Everyone has a bad hair day now and then, even Nancy—especially on days when she's fallen into a rushing stream, down a muddy embankment, or under a filthy chimney. But she bounces back quickly, as does her do, after a quick shower, shampoo, and set. Try these tricks for managing your own mane.

- **Fluff that five o'clock flat hair.** If you've been on the job all day, your hair may be somewhat droopy or downright flat. Mist it with a little water and shape it into place with your fingers. The water will activate the mousse, hairspray, or gel that's already in your hair, so you won't need to add more product.

- **Get the gray out— fast.** If you've got a little gray showing and need to cover it up quickly as part of your disguise, brush in a little mascara in a color that most closely matches your hair to camouflage the most obvious gray strands. If you're blonde or titian haired, spray in a temporary tint.

- **When you're out of mousse.** If you need to tame your tresses after a ride in your roadster or a chase after criminals, ask a male friend for a small amount of shaving cream for a quick fix.

- **When you need to repair a bad haircut.** If you're on the road and get a bad haircut, try styling it a new way, with hot curlers, mousse, or hairspray. Trim away any obvious stray strands but don't attempt to cut your own hair. Return to the salon as soon as possible and have them repair it.

- **When you're having a bad hair day.** If you just can't do a thing with your hair, wet it, add mousse, and try restyling it. If it's too stubborn to behave, cover it with a smart cloche hat or use a stylish scarf as a headband. Last but not least, pull it into a ponytail or give it a twist. Then stick a flower in it to draw attention away from the hair.

- **When your perm is botched.** Apply a deep conditioner each day and leave it on for fifteen minutes. Add a leave-in conditioner after shampooing and rinsing your hair. If, after two to three days, your hair is still a fright, see if a professional stylist can relax the perm. If all else fails, tie a scarf around your hair and wear sunglasses to get that mysterious Girl Detective look.

Look 18 When You're Not

No matter how old Nancy is, she always looks eighteen (unless she's disguised as an old lady). How does she keep that youthful glow? Sleuthing helps—it keeps her mind and body active and vibrant. Here are some tips to help keep you looking young no matter what your age.

1 Keep your hair just below the chin.

You don't have to wear your hair short just because you're a "mature" woman. What you want is a haircut that frames and flatters your face and draws attention away from signs of aging. Your hair should be cut to just below your jaw line, with the focus on the hair's texture, color, and volume to add youth to your look.

2 Add color to drab hair.

Gray hair is an obvious sign of aging that can easily be remedied. Choose a hair dye close to your original color so that it naturally complements your facial tones. Or add highlights or lowlights that add interest to your hair and don't require a lot of maintenance.

3 Choose your lip color with care.

The shade of your lipstick can also add years—or take them away. Avoid dark colors, like deep red and maroon, and shades of brown. Instead try pinks, corals, and cherry or scarlet. Be sure to outline your lips with lip liner to keep the color from bleeding into any lines around your mouth. Use gloss to add a subtle shimmer and protect against dry, cracked lips.

4 *Get your teeth whitened.*

A smile can take years off your face, while frowning causes wrinkles and makes you look older. So can coffee, tea, red wine, and nicotine. You can whiten your teeth with simple over-the-counter products. Between use, brush your teeth frequently with whitening toothpaste. If these products are not effective, see your dentist about whitening procedures.

5 *Get a good night's sleep.*

Nancy knows the value of a good night's sleep, especially when she's dealing with a particularly knotty problem or mystery. To avoid puffy eyes, sallow skin, and more facial lines, get at least eight solid hours of sleep. This will help you rejuvenate, and you'll feel better—and younger, too.

6 *Eat a healthy, nutritious diet.*

Nancy always eats well—moderate portions of steak, salads, fruits, and vegetables—and even indulges in small portions of dessert. Take the time to eat nutritious meals, and you'll look and feel better.

7 *Lose excess weight.*

While you're eating healthy, take smaller portions and avoid heavy desserts and fatty foods. Then watch the weight fall off as you feel better and look more youthful.

8 *Exercise regularly to maintain your shape and tone.*

There are lots of ways to stay in shape, aside from going to the gym. Nancy keeps herself firm and fit by engaging in all sorts of sports. Consider bike riding, horseback riding, archery, and skin diving or playing tennis, shuffleboard, and golf (as well as running after criminals, of course).

9 *Use a good-quality sunscreen.*

To avoid aging your skin and risking skin cancer, forego the sunbathing and avoid tanning booths. Instead, use a tanning lotion to give yourself a healthy and safe sun-kissed look.

10 *Choose the right clothes to complement your body.*

Don't try to look like an eighteen-year-old when you're not. Instead, wear flowing clothes in soft colors that are not too tight (so they don't show your bulges) or too loose (so you don't look frumpy). Avoid bold patterns, stripes, and odd colors. Remember, black is always slimming.

Stay Fit and Ready for Physical Challenges

Because she stays fit, Nancy is always in shape to chase a suspect or climb up a trellis. She makes exercising fun by engaging in her athletic passions: skin diving, swimming, shuffle boarding, and other aerobic and muscle-building sports. Staying in shape not only protects you from dangerous criminals, it also helps strengthen your body, boosts your immune system, and prevents certain diseases, like osteoporosis. Exercise helps you maintain flexibility, endurance, and strength. And it helps you feel good while reducing stress and increasing cognitive abilities.

1 Join a fitness club.

If you prefer a structured workout, consider joining a fitness club or gym. Make sure the instructors are qualified, the facilities are clean, and the equipment is well maintained.

2 Invest in the appropriate workout clothes or sports gear.

Exercise clothing and footwear should be comfortable. Shoes should have some cushion to absorb the impact of walking, running, or other aerobics, while your outfits should be loose and made from a natural fiber, like cotton, to allow your skin to breathe.

3 Set a realistic exercise schedule and stick to it.

Set a specific time for exercise and try to meet that commitment regularly. If you find you're getting not enough—or too much—exercise, adjust your schedule to fit your needs.

4 Pursue opportunities to learn new sports and activities.

Try a new sport that will sharpen your coordination and improve your concentration, such as snorkeling, canoeing, salsa dancing, badminton, croquet, or water skiing. Sports that rely on hand-eye coordination are ideal for working the brain as well as the body.

5 Include exercise in your daily life.

Make exercise a part of your daily routine, just like showering, eating, and sleuthing. Take every opportunity to move your body instead of remaining sedentary:

- Take the stairs.
- Walk to your destination.
- Engage in physical play with your pets or children.
- Clean your house instead of hiring someone to do it for you.
- Walk around the mall, airline terminal, or up and down the office stairs when the weather is inclement.

HOW TO

Employ the Etiquette Essentials

No matter how stressful a situation may be—tracking a kidnapper, rescuing a drowning victim, or attending a séance—proper manners and basic etiquette are always appreciated. Nancy and her friends know how to behave at any function—a tea, a party, a wedding, a restaurant gathering—and are welcome guests because of it.

Know how to comport yourself at tea.

Use your best manners, whether it's an informal cup with friends or a formal full-service high tea.

- Respond to the invitation promptly and be on time.
- Dress according to the weather, the local customs, the time of day, and the type of tea party. A nice frock or slacks out-fit is appropriate for indoors; outdoor teas are less formal, so a sundress or proper shorts would be acceptable. Find out whether gloves are required.
- If the tea is being hosted in someone's honor, be sure to bring an appropriate gift. Otherwise, offer a small token to the hostess of the party.
- Be sure to take note of proper tea etiquette: When drinking tea, raise the teacup, not the saucer, and return it to the saucer between sips. Keep your pinky finger up for balance as you hold the teacup handle; never grasp the cup itself or stick your finger through the handle. Don't

stir the tea; rather, fold the teaspoon into the cup several times. Sip, don't slurp. And don't leave the spoon in the cup; place it to the right of the saucer.

- Come prepared with interesting and entertaining topics to discuss with enthusiasm.

Be a proper, courteous restaurant guest.

Know which fork to use, how to pass the butter, and when to speak.

- Dress appropriately for the restaurant and occasion.
- Make sure you have money in case the cost is to be shared.
- Wait in the restaurant entryway if you're the first to arrive.
- Be polite, smile, and use your best manners.
- Know the basics of handling tableware: When the host unfolds her napkin, you do the same. Place it on your lap, completely unfolded. Keep it there (unless, of course, you're using it) until the end of the meal. Then place it on the table after your host does so. Don't refold it or wad it up.
- Learn proper silverware placement and use: On the right are the glassware, cup and saucer, knives, spoons, and seafood fork, if needed. On the left are the bread plate (with butter knife), salad plate, napkin, and forks. Start with the utensil that is farthest from your plate and work your way in. Never pick up a dropped utensil; ask your server for another.
- Be discreet about your dietary needs and pretend to enjoy the food, even if you don't. There should be something on the menu you can eat, even with the most restrictive diet.
- Don't order the most expensive items on the menu.
- While eating, keep pace with the rest of the guests.

- Use moderation in eating, drinking, laughing, and talking.
- Take part in the conversation, but don't bring up controversial or unpleasant topics.
- Never talk with your mouth full.
- Don't apply makeup at the table; rather, excuse yourself to the ladies' room.
- Upon taking your leave, thank everyone for the pleasant time.
- Tip the waitstaff 15 to 20 percent of the bill, depending on the service. Tip the coat checker one dollar per coat, on the way out, and the parking valet two dollars when he returns your car.

One never knows what secrets may
be revealed, even at a formal tea.

Be a gracious houseguest.

Nancy often spends the night at a mysterious inn or a haunted mansion. While tracking clues, she knows how to be a gracious guest.

- Pack the proper clothing and accessories, including any sleuthing or sports equipment you might need, such as a flashlight or scuba equipment.
- Make sure your luggage is not frayed, dirty, or broken.
- Do not bring along your pets, children, or boyfriend unless the host specifically asks.
- Bring a gift, such as a bottle of wine, a local delicacy, a houseplant, a candle, or other decorator item. If your host has children, bring something for them.
- Be complimentary of your accommodations, not critical. If you must ask for something that's not been supplied, do so as delicately as possible.
- Be extremely careful with your host's housewares, furniture, and knick-knacks. If you do break something, admit it, apologize, and offer to replace it.
- Be on time if your host has scheduled a local trip or event. And be enthusiastic about the plans.
- Clean up after yourself, including stripping the bed when the visit is over. (Ask permission first if there's any question about what you should do.)
- Treat your hosts to dinner at a nice restaurant while you're there.
- Leave when promised; don't wear out your welcome.
- Always write a thank-you note after you've returned home from the visit.

HOW TO

Arrange Prize-Winning Flowers

Nancy's talents extend beyond sports and sleuthing. She's also gifted at flower arranging and has won prizes for her displays. Nancy turns to flowers as a way of expressing her artistry, allowing her to clear away the cobwebs so she can return refreshed to solve a particularly complex mystery. Follow Nancy's prize-winning flower arrangement tips, and you'll soon have an exquisite display you can enter in the annual charity flower show.

1 *Choose flowers to suit the occasion.*

You can grow your own prize-winning flowers or buy them at your local grocery store or farmer's market. You don't need expensive blooms to create a beautiful bouquet—just a little creativity. Think about what you want to express with your display and what color scheme you'd like for the occasion. For example, you might want red roses for a Valentine's Day centerpiece, daisies for a summer picnic, or a spray of multi-colored blooms as a reward for solving a particularly challenging mystery.

2 *Trim the stems.*

Cut stalks of the finest flowers and soon you'll have a basketful. Soak the stems, then lay the flowers on the table and trim about half an inch off the bottom with a sharp knife or pruning shears. Do not use scissors—they pinch the ends and cut off the supply of water and oxygen. Cut the stems at an angle. For even better results, cut them in a sink full of water. Remove excess leaves and any thorns.

3 Select a vase and set the foundation.

Find a vase, about ten to fourteen inches tall, with a small-ish neck to hold your flower arrangement. Create a foundation for the flowers by placing a piece of green Styrofoam, clay, or small pebbles at the bottom of the vase. You can also use clear tape to create a grid across the top of the vase, running two pieces in a criss-cross direction. This will hold the flowers in place until the vase is filled; you'll remove the tape when you're done.

4 Choose your focal flower.

Select flowers that are similar or complementary colors, such as blue or lavender delphiniums and blue or mauve larkspur. The flowers should be half again as tall as the vase. Choose the fullest, best-looking flower for the center/front of your display. Trim the stem so it's shorter than the rest of the flowers.

5 Fill in around the focal point.

- Choose the tallest flower next, and place it in the middle of the vase.
- Hold four more flowers in the vase to size them, then trim them so they're shorter than the tallest flower. Place them around the center flower, spaced equally apart.
- Measure and trim seven more flowers so they're shorter than the others. Fill in the vase, equally spacing the flowers.

6 *Add finishing touches.*

Add sprigs of greenery, baby's breath, rice flower, statice, goldenrod, leaf fern, or other filler to close the gaps between flowers and create fullness. Cut them shorter than the flowers so they don't obscure them. Consider adding lengths of ribbon for a festive look and added color. Be careful not to overload the arrangement with too much, or you'll ruin the effect.

7 *Stand back.*

Take a look at the display from a short distance to make sure it looks attractive and that there are no holes. Check the distribution of color so that it's pleasing to the eye and the focal point to ensure that it's still dominant. Lastly, fill in any areas that need more greenery.

8 *Add water and food.*

Fill the vase three-quarters with tepid water, and add flower food to prolong the plant's beauty. (If you don't have flower food, add 1 tablespoon of sugar and 1 tablespoon of bleach to the water.) Remember to change the water every two days, and trim the stems every four to five days to keep them fresh. Keep your display away from warm areas, such as in sunlight, near a heater, or on top of the television.

9 *Enter your arrangement in a local flower show.*

With Nancy's tips for flower arranging, you have an excellent chance of winning first prize!

CHAPTER 3

Detecting Clues

Be a Good Sleuth and Gather Important Clues to Solve a Mystery

Nancy started to laugh. "Hold it! As detectives, we must not get carried away with guesses. Let's try to find out the facts!"—Mystery of the Brass-Bound Trunk

It's a sense of adventure that draws Nancy Drew to detecting. What makes her such a good sleuth are her abilities to focus on the facts, observe the smallest details, understand a person's behavior, and reason without letting emotion take over. Of course, these skills would make her good at anything she pursued, not just detecting. Here are some pointers for following in Nancy's footsteps.

1 Make a master plan.

If you stumble upon a mystery you want to solve, take time to study the facts and create a plan of action. Learn as much as you can about the crime, the victims and suspects, and, finally, the motive. Then brainstorm all possibilities for solving the mystery, along with backup plans, escape routes, and other contingencies.

2 Gather all necessary supplies.

A resourceful detective never leaves home without the proper tools of her trade. Most of the items can be carried in an oversized handbag, making them available for use at all times, especially in an emergency. (See "How to Pack the Perfect Handbag for All Contingencies," page 28.)

3 Be cool, not obvious.

If you try to act like a detective, you'll only draw attention to yourself. Instead of donning a costume, such as sunglasses, a trench coat, and a fedora, it's better to blend in and look like everyone else. You're likely to get a lot more information that way.

4 Organize your team.

George and Bess, Nancy's two best friends, are always there for backup to help her when she's in a tight spot. Even Ned and his buddies join the gang from time to time, which makes investigating even more fun. It's best to have friends who have other skills you don't possess, such as knowledge of judo. Give the team members code names, assign them tasks, and don't hesitate to call on them when you're in trouble. Remember, there's safety in numbers, so include the team on your more dangerous tasks, and never investigate a mystery alone.

5 Gather intelligence.

Before you begin your mission and set your plan in motion, gather information about the crime, the suspects, the victims, and the scene. You can scout out the surroundings for any hidden passageways, make maps of the area, and plan escape routes. Canvass the neighborhood and interview witnesses, take statements, and verify credentials. (A tip from Nancy: Ask the local postal carrier where a suspect lives.)

6 Expand your communication resources.

There are a number of ways Nancy communicates with her pals when she's investigating a dangerous mystery, especially when she doesn't want a suspect to overhear her plans.

- Write your message on paper instead of speaking it aloud to prevent others from overhearing you.
- Use odd wording when you write a note to alert the reader there's a hidden message.
- Leave a personal object along your path to let your friends know when you've been abducted or are in trouble.
- Learn Morse code and tap out messages with your heels. (See page 124.)
- Learn Sign Language to talk privately with your hands.

7 Cultivate an eye for detail.

Practice observing people, objects, and your surroundings, and you'll begin to spot clues others have overlooked. Sometimes a clue is in plain sight, so don't forget to consider the obvious. You never know when you might find something in an old diary, a collection of model ships, a style of handwriting, or a pair of muddy shoes.

8 Learn to read faces and body language.

Nancy can tell by a person's shifty eyes or cruel smile that he's not to be trusted. She also looks at body language for signs of criminal traits. Practice watching people's facial expressions and body movements to see if you can detect hidden signs of good or evil character.

9 *Keep careful notes of your investigation.*

Always have pen and paper handy to jot down character traits, reproduce footprints, draw maps, pass secret information, produce sketches of suspects, or simply record details of your investigation.

10 *Go with your hunches.*

Nancy's hunches almost always turn out to be accurate. Some of us are not so intuitive, but if your gut is trying to tell you something, listen to it. It may keep you from danger or help you solve a crime.

11 *Work with the police.*

Nancy never obstructs justice, harbors fugitives, keeps stolen property, enters unlawfully, or breaks the law, unless it's absolutely necessary. Whenever possible, she calls the police to alert them of a crime or a dangerous situation, and she makes every effort to stay in good standing with law enforcement personnel.

12 *Be wary and stay safe at all times.*

Be especially careful when snooping in old attics, castle dungeons, secret passageways, hidden staircases, moss-covered mansions, and dark alleys. Remember: Even a sleepy tree-lined suburban town can be a hotbed of criminal activity, concealing everyone from burglars and jewel thieves to smugglers, kidnappers, and organized crime syndicates.

Disguise Yourself and Go Undercover

"We must make our plans carefully. Before we do anything, I suggest we find out about the robes the cult members wear. We may need to wear similar ones to help us in our investigation. I think we'll be able to make costumes like theirs if you'll give us some old pillowcases and sheets, Jo," Nancy said.—The Secret of Red Gate Farm

Since Nancy has become quite famous for her detecting skills, she sometimes finds it necessary to don a disguise so she can carry out her investigations. If you find yourself in a situation where you need to obscure your identity, assume another identity, disappear, or go undercover, try the following suggestions.

- **Dress for the situation.** If you're investigating a cult, you can easily turn old sheets and pillowcases into appropriate costumes and blend in at their secret meetings. If you're planning to spy on a suspected crime syndicate, you'll need to look like a mob moll, with overdone make-up, big hair, short skirt, and low-cut blouse. If there's a mystery brewing at a dude ranch, find yourself a pair of boots, a hat, and a cute bandanna to use as a disguise.

- **Wear multi-functional clothes.** If possible, buy reversible trench coats, long pants that unzip into shorts, or layered tops so you can make a quick change when you don't want to be spotted.

- **Don a wig.** Wigs do wonders for changing one's appearance. Try various looks to match your purpose: a blonde wig if you're investigating in Hollywood or a mousy brunette wig if you're undercover as a librarian. To age yourself dramatically, wear a gray wig with a blue rinse tinge to it.
- **Add distracting accessories.** Accessories are a must when it comes to disguises. Dark glasses are de rigueur to avoid being recognized or spotted. A scarf provides an easy way to change your appearance and can be used in several different ways—tied around your hair, arranged around your neck, or secured as a headband. Other accessories include frumpy shoes, a knitted shawl, a trench coat, a cloche hat, and a dark veil.

It's important to blend in when undercover.

- **Change your skin color.** Lather on quick-tanning lotion for an exotic look, then add freckles, a mole, or a scar using an eyebrow pencil.
- **Age yourself.** No disguise works better than the "Little Old Lady" look. Check your mother's or grandmother's closet for a dated outfit, don old shoes, then top it off by dusting your hair with gray powder. (Alternatively, use a color rinse or wear a wig.) Enhance the look with sagging stockings, wire-rimmed glasses, and a crocheted shawl. Then hunch yourself over and practice speaking in a croaky voice.
- **Assume an alias.** Choose a name that fits your assumed character, then have fake business cards, stationery, identity cards, even credit cards made to confirm your false identity. If anyone should suspect you're not whom you say you are, simply hand them a card or show them your fake ID.
- **Pose as hired help to blend in.** People tend not to notice others who seem to be a part of their surroundings, such as hired help or temporary staff. Accordingly, this is one of the most effective ways to disappear in plain view and gather evidence. Some of the best occupations for undercover work include:

    Waiter—wear a black outfit with a white apron and carry a tray

    Medical staff—wear a white doctor's coat and carry a stethoscope

    Wedding guest—wear a dressy outfit and carry a glass of champagne

    Administrative assistant—wear a business suit and carry a clipboard

    Cleaning company personnel—wear overalls and carry a dust rag

Follow a Suspect Unobserved

Whether it's an evil mastermind trying to set off a bomb, a suspicious character claiming to be a prince, or your scheming boyfriend who may be cheating on you, you can follow anyone unobserved if you know the tricks of the trade. The key to tailing a suspect is the ability to become invisible. The main thing to remember is the axiom: "Don't Get Caught." Easier said than done. Tailing is a "reactive" skill—the subject acts, and you react.

1 *Blend in with your surroundings.*

Avoid bright colors, bare midriffs, low-rise jeans, or a frock you normally wear to draw attention to yourself. Now is not the time to make a fashion statement. Instead, wear plain black from head to toe: black jeans and a black scarf, along with black tennis shoes for chasing the suspect and a black backpack for storing stakeout snacks and surveillance supplies.

2 *Tailor your outfit to match the environment.*

If you're tailing a suspicious cowboy, wear boots and a stylish bandanna, not Jimmy Choos and an Hermès scarf. If you're in the city, don a fashionable coat, cloche hat, and designer sunglasses to blend in. Avoid obvious disguises, like dirty trench coats, Groucho Marx glasses, or T-shirts that say "I ♥ Ned."

3 Become familiar with your suspect's appearance.

Be observant. Begin by knowing your subject well—especially what he looks like from behind, since that's the angle you'll see the most. Study his walk, clothing, and footprints, so you can spot him from a distance, at a crowded party, or in a men's room stall.

4 Use caution when following a possible criminal.

Be smart when tailing a suspect. Don't follow too closely behind or he could turn around and assault you. Don't look into shop windows every time the suspect turns around—that just makes you look suspicious. If he does spot you, keep moving down the street instead of constantly ducking into alleyways.

5 Remain unobtrusive when following a suspect.

Try not to look at the suspect directly. Instead, use your peripheral vision, compact mirrors, window reflections, periscopes, or holes cut in newspapers to watch him. Maintain a close enough distance so that you won't lose the tail, but not so close that you're likely to be spotted. For example, if you're in a crowd, you can stay in close proximity. But if there are few people in the area, maintain as much distance as possible.

6 *Maintain your anonymity when following in a car.*

If your suspect takes off in a vehicle, don't take the blue roadster—it may attract unwanted attention. Borrow an inconspicuous car with no gunshot marks, funny bumpers stickers, or "Just Married" signs. If you're tailing the suspect at night, drive with your lights off, but always make sure you've fastened your seatbelt.

7 *Be prepared for a stakeout.*

If your suspect enters a building, you may be stuck in your car for quite a while. Take along a variety of healthy snacks, magazines, and your radio to keep occupied. Bring your camera to take photographic evidence and your cell phone or carrier pigeon (see "How to Train a Carrier Pigeon," page 85) to contact other operatives or your sidekicks.

8 *Be ready if you get caught.*

If you should get "made" or "burned"—accidentally come face to face with the suspect—don't panic. Remember, you have the advantage since you know you're following him, but he probably doesn't, at least not for sure. Be prepared with a plausible lie to cover yourself, such as "I was shopping," "looking for my lost dog," or "just curious."

9 *If you lose your suspect, call it a day.*

When Nancy loses her suspect, she simply begins anew the next time she spots him. Investigate the area, question bystanders, and put your ear to the ground to pick up the trail.

HOW TO

Tell When Someone Is Lying

Although Nancy has a sixth sense for determining whether a person is lying, you don't need a lie detector to know someone is trying to deceive. There are many ways to spot a dishonest suspect and get him to reveal the truth.

1 Study his body language.

Look for the following signs:

- Darting eyes, dilated pupils, increased blinking
- Crosses arms and/or legs, stiffening of body
- Fidgety or nervous behavior, lowers his head, turns away
- Flushed or pale face
- Dry mouth, tight lips, clenched jaw, hand covers mouth
- Shallow or rapid breathing

2 Listen for inconsistencies.

Listen for these signs as you interview a suspect:

- Talks rapidly, in a hurry to get the interrogation over with
- Mumbles, speaks in vague terms
- Mispronounces words, says "No" when he means "Yes"
- Forgets details, adds something new, mixes things up
- Body language and facial expression don't match words
- Overly friendly, laughing, wants you to like him
- Trying to sound casual when he's not
- Clears his throat, asks you to repeat the question

③ *Watch for defensiveness.*

Watch for the culprit to do the following:

- Be argumentative
- Turn hostile
- Refuse to answer questions
- Stammer
- Change the subject
- Accuse you of lying
- Shout
- Claim that his rights are being violated
- Blame others

④ *Use your intuition.*

Tap into your own natural resources when you feel someone may not be telling the whole truth. Don't jump to conclusions, but do listen to your gut. Then gather evidence to confirm your suspicion.

⑤ *Give him the opportunity to tell the truth.*

Sometimes the criminal just wants to confess. Question him directly. You may be surprised to find that he quickly comes clean.

⑥ *Be sympathetic.*

A liar is more likely to be truthful if you try to empathize with him and understand his motives for committing the crime. If he trusts your sincerity, he may spill the beans.

Analyze Handwriting

Nancy is intrigued by the study of graphology and is astute at deciphering the character of criminals through their script. She can often tell when someone has deliberately tried to alter his handwriting to throw off suspicion. Scientists believe one's handwriting is a clue to one's personality, character—even soul. Here are some tips to help you analyze the scribblings of your friends and foes, to understand their traits and quirks—and see if they possess any criminal traits.

1 Study graphology.

Take a course in graphology, or handwriting analysis. Proper identification of the strokes, patterns, and variations in pressure can reveal a lot about a person's intelligence, emotions, fears, and imagination, opening a window into the subconscious mind.

2 Get a handwriting sample.

Collect a sample from a golf scorecard, hotel registration, or blank sheet of paper left in the upraised hand of a marble statue. Use it as a sample for analysis to determine more about a suspect. He may be trying to disguise his handwriting for nefarious purposes, such as forgery.

③ Note the dominant features.

See if you can obtain an overall feeling for the person first by looking generally at his handwriting. The dominant features represent the foremost characters of the subject's personality. If the script is small, it may represent a person who is socially reserved. If the handwriting is large and flamboyant, it may indicate the person wants attention.

④ Analyze the closeness and pressure of letters.

If the handwriting is cramped, tight, and lower-case, this may reflect an introverted person. If the script is bold, upper-case, or spread out, these are signs of extroversion. If a suspect deliberately tries to obscure his handwriting, he may be fearful someone will recognize it and that it may lead to his arrest.

⑤ Look at the pressure of the writing.

If the writing is dark, it indicates a lot of pressure and high energy. If it's light, the opposite is true. People who exert heavy pressure tend to be successful, while those with light pressure tend not to challenge themselves.

⑥ Pay attention to the slant.

A right slant indicates a subject who responds to emotional situations. He tends to be caring, warm, and outgoing. A vertical slant generally means he keeps his emotions under control. And a left slant usually suggests the person suppresses his emotions and is cold and uncaring.

7 *Look for graphic gestures.*

Don't overlook handwriting decorations, such as doodles, flowers, smiley faces, etc. These can reveal a lot about personality as well. For example, if a person doodles aimlessly, his mind may be elsewhere or he might be dealing with stress.

8 *Try not to make assumptions.*

Many samples of handwriting show contradictions, so you need to take into account mitigating factors before you draw conclusions. As when solving a mystery, you'll need to study all the evidence, then come to a decision regarding which character traits are salient to the individual you are analyzing.

vertical slant indicates
controlled emotions

lowercase indicates
introversion

heavy pressure
indicates high energy

Analyze Suspicious Footprints

Nancy never overlooks suspicious footprints. She can often tell a lot about the suspect just by carefully checking the dirt for telltale signs of a trespasser. If you're trailing a suspect's footprints, or find suspicious footprints under your bedroom window, here are some things you can deduce that will help you identify the wearer.

1 Measure the footprint.

The length of a person's foot is approximately 15 percent of his or her height. A heavier imprint indicates a hefty person, whereas a light step usually means a slim person. The length of the stride can tell you whether the suspect is running or walking or has been injured.

2 Examine the sole design for clues.

Shoes leave unique prints based on the sole design, which can generally be narrowed down to just one shoe manufacturer. In cases where the shoe design is exclusive and sold in select footwear establishments, the shoe owner's identity can be traced by means of store receipts. (Note that shoe manufacturers also submit information regarding the patterns on soles to law-enforcement laboratories, and the information is computerized.)

Examine the pattern of wear on the shoe.

A seasoned footprint analyst will also be able to determine the characteristic walk or gait of the person, the unique sole or heel indents, and the cuts or tread of a shoe based on nothing more than a single print. When these prints are matched with a suspect, you have your crook.

4 Preserve your findings.

Photographs or castings of footprints can be taken to preserve the evidence. In the event you have not made an initial exact match between footprint and subject, you'll have a visual record to make a subsequent positive match. Footprints are not as unique as a fingerprint or DNA evidence, but they can be enough for a criminal conviction.

Locate a Secret Passageway

During her investigations, Nancy often discovers a secret passageway. And just as often this hidden passage leads to danger—and the solution to the mystery. Secret passageways are more plentiful than most people realize. You may have one in your home or office building, or you might find one in a local deserted mansion or abandoned inn. Throughout history, hidden rooms and passageways have been used to keep people safe, help them escape capture, or even hide illegal activities, such as smuggling or operating speakeasies. Today, some people have hidden passageways that lead to "panic rooms" constructed to keep them safe in case of a break-in. Here are some ways to help you uncover a hidden passageway in your own home or a nearby castle.

1 Look for a camouflaged entryway.

A secret entryway is usually disguised by a camouflaged door, so it looks like part of the wall, bookcase, or fireplace. Use the heel of your shoe, a hammer, or your knuckles to rap along the wall and listen for a hollow sound that would indicate a hidden passageway or room. Also look for any mismatched wallpaper seams, uneven paint lines, or gaps between bookcases.

2 Consider the presence of a trap door.

Some hidden passageways and rooms are located beneath trap doors. These are usually easier to find, since most people simply cover them with throw rugs, heavy appliances, or antique armoires. Use caution when searching for a trap door; it may suddenly give way when you stand on it.

3 Check for a sliding panel.

Sliding panels are excellent devices for hiding rooms and passageways. There are no obvious seams, knobs, or buttons, yet the wall slides open when the operator knows the secret. Tap and listen for that hollow sound, then search for the catch-release mechanism. (See "Locating a Catch-Release Mechanism," opposite.)

Catch-release mechanisms are sometimes
disguised as mundane objects.

Locating a Catch-Release Mechanism

Some camouflaged entryways are difficult to discover because they can be opened only by triggering a concealed button or locking mechanism. Once you think you've found a hidden doorway, look around for a device that might activate it:

• a brass candlestick that appears to be bolted to the mantel
• fireplace tools that are never used
• a button hidden behind a large portrait on the wall

4 Be prepared to force your way in.

If you can't find any other way to enter the passageway, and it's a matter of life or death, then you may have to force it open. It's helpful to have a couple of young men available to do this, but if you're alone, try ramming your shoulder at the door, throwing a chair at it, beating the door with a fireplace tool, or prying it open with golf shoe cleats.

5 Be ready for small spaces.

Once you find the opening, you may be surprised to see how small the passageway really is. Most are tight and small to avoid discovery. Make sure you can fit through the space before attempting to investigate, or you may find yourself trapped inside!

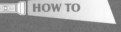

Open a Locked Trunk

Nancy often finds valuable treasures or the key to a mystery inside a locked trunk, antique jewel box, or secret compartment of a statue. But it takes some clever deduction to figure out how to open it when you don't have a key. You can, of course, call a locksmith. He's a trained professional and can open most locks, as long as he's not asked to do anything illegal. But when a locksmith is not an option, you'll need to use your ingenuity and know-how.

1 Familiarize yourself with basic lock technology.

The pin-and-tumbler lock consists of a cylinder that can rotate within its housing. When locked, the cylinder is kept in place by several pairs of pins. When the correct key is inserted, it pushes the pairs of pins up so that the top pins no longer enter the cylinder. Then the cylinder can be turned and the lock will open.

2 Invest in basic lock-picking tools.

Most locks are simple pin-and-tumbler assemblies and can be relatively easy to open using a pick and tension wrench. Each pick is specialized for a different problem. A tension wrench, or torque wrench, is the device with which you apply pressure to turn the lock cylinder. Professional-grade picks and tension wrenches can be purchased in sets.

HOW TO OPEN A LOCKED TRUNK

③ Practice picking simple locks.

When you turn the cylinder, it will turn only a fraction of an inch before it stops. Feel the firmness of the stop. If you turn the cylinder the wrong way, the stop should feel firm. If you turn it the right way, there should be more give.

- Apply light torque to the tension wrench in the correct direction and hold.
- Insert the pick into the upper part of the keyhole, press up, and feel the individual pins. Push them up and feel them spring back down when you release the pressure.
- Use the tension wrench to turn the cylinder and unlock the lock.
- Once all the pins are set, turn the cylinder to open it.

④ Improvise when you don't have the right tools.

If you don't have your picks handy, use a paperclip or safety pin to push up and release the lock's pins.

⑤ If all else fails, break open the trunk.

If you don't have a crowbar or skeleton key, be creative: Try opening the lock using a nail file, a hammer, or the cleats on your golf shoes when you're in a pinch.

⑥ Once you've opened the trunk, check for secret compartments.

Measure the trunk, inside and out, to see if there are any discrepancies in size—a sure sign of a hidden compartment. Run your fingers along the inside panels to see if you can feel a false side or bottom. Check the lining as well; it can also hide secret contents.

Uncover a "Haunted" Bungalow and Other Ghostly Apparitions

Bess has always been easily frightened, but her pal Nancy knows there are no such things as ghosts—and she often has to prove it. If you suspect you're the victim of a "haunting," and feel a chill running down your spine, dispel the fraud with the following steps.

1 Locate the site of the disturbance.

Thoroughly investigate the bungalow, mansion, castle, or cottage to determine where the "ghost" is residing, or where it's doing most of its "haunting." Check behind secret panels, under trap doors, inside neglected closets, and, of course, in the dusty old attic.

2 Research the site for clues.

Check into the background of the building and the area in which it resides. You may find that the site was once a Native American burial ground, the scene of a heinous murder, or a place where treasure was buried.

82

3 Determine what kind of "ghost" it is.

The field of parapsychology recognizes three kinds of events related to "ghosts":

- Those that haunt places where special events have occurred. These ghosts are usually benign and not interactive.
- Those that are made by a poltergeist. These ghosts are characterized by moving objects and strange sounds and images, caused subconsciously by a person under a lot of stress.
- Those that are apparitions of dead people. These sightings are extremely rare, and have not been proved, although encounters seem to be interactive.

4 Gather a team to assist you.

Something or someone is most likely causing the disturbance, so it would be foolish to investigate the property alone. Choose a team of friends, law enforcement personnel, or paranormal investigators to accompany you on your visits to the haunted site.

5 Assemble your equipment.

You'll need a few basic pieces of equipment if you want to prove a site is not haunted:

- Notebook and pen to record suspicious details.
- Tape recorder or video camera to obtain "proof."
- Compass to test for electromagnetic field.
- Infrared thermometer to pick up temperature changes.
- First-aid kit, in case the "ghost" attacks you.
- Food, drinks, and sleeping bags for a long stakeout.
- Geiger counter to register paranormal events.

6 *Sweep the area.*

Take the time to make another search of the area to look for obvious signs of fraud and fakery.

7 *Gather the data.*

Set up cameras to record suspicious events. Write down everything you see and hear so no one can accuse you of having a wild imagination. Include the date, time, location, sounds, sights, smells, temperature, weather, and anything else you think might be helpful to prove your case.

8 *Try to be an "open-minded skeptic."*

People see what they want to see. If they believe in ghosts, they'll probably "see" a ghost. But there's always something behind the "haunting" that you'll need to uncover. Rule out other possibilities of the disturbance until you find the most likely cause.

9 *Don't panic, but be prepared to duck.*

Ghosts cannot hurt you. Even in cases of poltergeist activity, most objects thrown through the air can be easily dodged if you keep your head about you. There's always a logical explanation for the disturbance, and once it's discovered, the mystery will be solved.

Train a Carrier Pigeon

Capsules for messages lay on a shelf. She took a pencil and small pad from her blouse pocket and wrote three identical messages: "SP at once." Nancy inserted them in the capsules, then caught a pigeon and attached the capsule to its anklet. "Fly straight to Ned," she muttered. —The Password to Larkspur Lane

Sure, every girl detective uses a cell phone, texting, and IM these days. But you never know when your techno-gadgets will fall out of your handbag, run out of batteries, or simply die on you. For backup, it's a good idea to have a low-tech solution on hand. Trained carrier pigeons are invaluable when it comes to sending secret messages that escape detection. How they are able to navigate is a mystery; some speculate that they orient themselves using the Earth's magnetic fields or by the positions of the sun and stars. The important thing is, they don't have to ask for directions.

1 *Find a reliable source.*

Contact the National Pigeon Association for referrals to reputable carrier pigeon merchants. (Their Web site, www.npausa.com, sells adorable pins and patches that would look great on a blouse or vest.) Or look for carrier pigeon nests hidden in crevices, rock cliffs, or barns.

2 Select the right pigeon.

Look for a healthy pigeon descended from a rock dove. They come in only one color—roadster blue—but you can find some accessorized with yellow, purple, and green feathers. Be sure to get a female pigeon (males tend to be more stubborn).

3 Provide proper care and feeding.

Pigeons eat twice a day—once in the morning and once at night—usually seeds, grains, leaves, and popcorn kernels, plus a little grit for digestion. They must be kept clean and healthy, and they require regular vaccinations to ward off worms and diseases. Place drinking water and bathing water in separate bowls. For easy cage cleanup, use a hand-held vacuum cleaner.

4 Train your pigeon to perch.

Begin the training when your pigeon is two to three months old, after she begins to perch on top of the coop. Use slow movements, and whistle or shake a feeding can while offering treats from your open palm. Soon your pigeon will trust you enough to step onto your finger.

5 *Take your pigeon for training flights.*

Before the morning feeding time, put your pigeon in a nice, well-ventilated crate. Drive about a mile from your home and release your pigeon. She will find her way back to her food source—your home base. Continue this several times a week, working up to five miles, then ten, and so on. Your carrier pigeon is considered fully trained when she's six months old and returns home from a forty-mile distance. (Keep in mind that, once your pigeon is trained, she's basically impossible to get rid of.)

6 *Attach a message to your carrier pigeon.*

At this point, your "homer" is ready to carry secret messages from any location away from its home base. Write your message in code on a small piece of paper or use microfilm. Roll it up, insert it in a small canister or capsule (called a "post"), and gently attach it to the pigeon's leg with a specially made snap-on band. Remember, the pigeon will return only to the home nest where he's been trained.

Note Choose a name for your pigeon that best fits his personality. Today's most popular bird names are Crackers, Feathers, Hootie, Lucky, Perky, Roadrunner, Solo, Tinkerbell, Tweety, and Woodstock. Avoid derogatory names, such as Birdbrain, Catfood, and Stoolie.

Decipher a Coded Message

Nancy is brilliant at recognizing and breaking codes. She's studied a lot about ciphers and codes and even learned Morse code, which she's used to tap out a message with the heel of her shoe. If you read or overhear something that seems to have a pattern but doesn't make sense, it may be a code. Here are some code-cracking basics.

1 Practice breaking easy codes.

The best way to learn how to crack a code is to practice creating and breaking your own. Gather your sidekicks and create codes for one another, then try to break them. Move on to harder codes as you become good at the easy ones.

2 Try basic number codes.

Number codes and alphanumeric codes that use both letters and numbers were frequently used by the military in wartime for secret communication. Write down the alphabet on a sheet of paper. Write the numbers from 1 to 26 underneath the letters so that each letter has a corresponding number. (See example, opposite.) Write a note substituting the corresponding numbers for letters and see if your friend can figure out the coded message. You can also write the alphabet in reverse, to make the code more difficult.

1	2	3	4	5	6	7	8	9	10	11	12	13
a	b	c	d	e	f	g	h	i	j	k	l	m

14	15	16	17	18	19	20	21	22	23	24	25	26
n	o	p	q	r	s	t	u	v	w	x	y	z

Example: 3-15-13-5   1-20   15-14-3-5
Decoded: Come at once

3 Study popular word codes.

Many codes are based on letters rather than numbers and can be designed in numerous ways. The most popular is the Reverse Alphabet Code. Write the alphabet on a sheet of paper. Underneath, write the alphabet in reverse, with each letter corresponding to another letter. (See example, below.) Then write a message using the code.

a	b	c	d	e	f	g	h	i	j	k	l	m	n	o	p	q	r	s	t	u	v	w	x	y	z
z	y	x	w	v	u	t	s	r	q	p	o	n	m	l	k	j	i	h	g	f	e	d	c	b	a

Example: x-z-o-o   k-l-o-r-x-v
Decoded: Call police

4 Learn Morse code.

Most code breakers know Morse code. It's easy to learn, easy to use, and works well as a form of communication when you are gagged and can't talk, or you don't have pen and paper. (See "How to Tap Out a Morse Code Message with Your High-Heeled Shoes," page 124.)

5 Be familiar with other forms of code.

A code can take many forms. Nancy once figured out messages that were hidden within a coat of arms, a line of Shakespeare, a poem by Chaucer, and many others. Messages can be sent using semaphore—flags that are held in various ways to signal from a distance. You can also use Braille or American Sign Language when you want to communicate privately or silently. Today text messaging is a popular form of coded communication, but requires a cell phone and IM capability.

6 Be creative when using codes in emergency situations.

When you're tied up, but still have at least some use of your hands, locate your handbag and pull out your powder compact. Flash the mirror glass toward the sun to signal for a rescue. Always carry a flashlight when you need to signal from a window in an emergency. If all else fails, use an animal sound known to you and your sidekicks as an emergency signal: Bark like a dog or hoot like an owl to tell them to get help, fast!

7 Keep your mind sharp by doing puzzles.

Nancy practices her craft by solving crosswords and doing other mind games. Stay sharp by working anagrams, acrostics, sudoku puzzles, and other mental challenges in your spare time.

CHAPTER 4

Clues to Love & Romance

Tell When a Man Is Attracted to You

"You came to see if I could give you a clue?" Fred was tall, spare, and strong-muscled, with a youthful face. His bright blue eyes sparkled boyishly. —The Secret of the Old Clock

Nancy Drew is great at reading people. When a man's "bright blue eyes sparkle boyishly," she knows he's interested. For the rest of us, it may not be so easy. Deducing whether or not a guy is attracted to you is often a mystery, but once you recognize the clues, it's easy to detect his degree of interest. Here are some ways to tell if he's fond of you.

1 Assess his mirroring technique.

When you're out with a suitor, watch his body language to assess his level of interest. He should do something called "mirroring": subtly (but subconsciously) imitating your actions, such as leaning in close when you lean in, taking a sip of his drink when you sip, or touching his hair when you run your fingers through your own titian tresses.

2 Watch for an increase in the frequency of his blinks.

The normal blink rate for humans is about 20 closures per minute, but scientists have found that blink rates accelerate during arousal, much in the way physiological responses are triggered during a lie detector test. To test your date's response, increase your own blink rate, and see if he does the same.

Note Don't confuse a "blink" with an "eyelash flutter," in which the lid moves rapidly but does not completely close. Your date may be uncomfortable with something you've said and respond with a lie, indicated by eyelash flutter rather than the full closure of a blink.

3 Watch his eyes for further clues.

His pupils will dilate if he's attracted to you and will constrict if he's not. The more your date likes you, the more his gaze will casually check out your body. Occasional glances at your mouth are also clues that he's intrigued.

Note If your date maintains eye contact too long—that is, he just stares at you—he may be pretending to listen while planning ways to take advantage of you.

4 Read his brow.

Eyebrows aren't just dust catchers. They're great clues to romantic interest. If your date exhibits a lot of up and down eyebrow movement, called "eyebrow flash," he's most likely fascinated by you. If he prolongs an eyebrow raise, he's definitely sending out a signal of attraction.

5 *Assess his proximity as an indicator of interest.*

The closer to you that your date sits or stands, the more interested he is. If you find him leaning in over a table, he's trying to get closer—not only physically, but romantically. Watch for gestures with his hands (such as reaching toward you), his head (such as nodding), or his body (such as leaning in your direction). These are all subconscious signals that he wants more contact.

6 *Assess his touch.*

Your date's first touch is critical, even though it may seem casual or accidental. If his hand touches a neutral part of your body, such as your arm or shoulder, he's checking to see if you will accept the contact. Touching you is a way of capturing your full attention and helps him figure out whether you're as interested as he is.

Note If his touch is inappropriate and he refuses to take your "no" as "no," you are well within your rights to slap him or say sharply, "Stop that!"

Tell a Good Guy from a Bad Guy

Nancy has a sixth sense when it comes to sniffing out a bad guy. There's always something about him that gives away his nasty secret; underneath that nice suit and hair pomade lurks a man with underhanded plans. It could be his wild bushy hair, his shifty, penetrating eyes, or his crude, scowling face. Whatever it is, Nancy spots them easily. If you lack that intuition, pay attention to these general rules.

- **A good guy makes plans in advance; a bad guy leaves it to the last minute.** If a man really cares about you, he'll make an effort to plan a nice evening, with dinner at a charming restaurant, a picnic in the park, or tickets to the latest musical theater. If he doesn't, he'll most likely have little to offer in the way of a date, aside from a quick bite at a cheap diner or front row seats at the movie house.
- **A good guy calls when he says he'll call; a bad guy doesn't.** No one likes to wait by the phone, and frankly, Nancy simply does not have time for that. If a man is sincere when he says he'll call, then he will, unless something life-threatening comes up or he's in serious danger. And if he doesn't call, then he's not the type to take home to father.
- **A good guy takes an active role in sharing your life; a bad guy only pretends to be involved.** If it's all about him—how long

he works out, how much money he makes, how well he plays golf, how important he is—that's a clear sign he's Mr. Wrong. Mr. Right is more interested in finding out about you and your life than in bragging about his accomplishments.

- **A good guy shares similar interests; a bad guy just isn't interested.** When you talk to him about things you care about, such as saving those in trouble, helping the less fortunate, righting a wrong, or overturning a miscarriage of justice, does he have similar values? Ask his views on religion, politics, or world issues to see if they match yours.

- **A good guy is honest; a bad guy leads a double life.** If you suspect your man is not who he appears to be, do some investigating to find out the truth. For example, if he never takes you home, perhaps he still lives with his mother. If he doesn't let you call him at the office, perhaps he doesn't really have a job. And if his ring finger has a mark or tan line, he's probably married.

Good guy   Bad guy

- **A good guy is in sync with you; a bad guy's timing is off.** If your lifestyles are very different, the relationship probably won't work. For example, if you're an early bird and he's a night owl, he may not understand that a girl needs her beauty sleep if she's to be a success in life. If he wants a big night on the town while you prefer a quiet evening by the fire, find someone who's better in sync with your life.

- **A good guy is there for you; a bad guy is unavailable.** A man should be eager to spend time with you. If the man you're dating is too busy, too tired, or travels too much to see you, he's probably not the one for you. He may be busy all the time because he's a workaholic, tired because he sees other women, or gone because he's got a whole other life.

Warning Bells

In sleuthing, as in romance, primary evidence will tip you off to whether you're dealing with a good guy or a bad guy:

- *You can spot a villain by his piercing dark eyes or small, shifty penetrating eyes, his stocky build, his coarse, stiff hair, and his severe, square-jawed face.*
- *Beware of anyone who has an evil or cruel glint, sallow skin, or a crinkly ear.*
- *Be on the lookout for villains wearing ill-fitting dirty clothes, flashy patterns, loud plaids, and gaudy neckties with grease spots.*
- *Watch out for men with strange names, like Rudy Raspin, Tom Tozzle, Mr. Warte, Grumper, Stumpy Dowd, Kit Kadle, Sniggs, Snorky, and Red Buzby.*

Determine a Man's Character by the Shoes He Wears

As the girls sat down, Dave and Shorty came in. Nancy glanced at their boots. There was damp red mud on both pairs! Once he caught Nancy looking at his shoes. "Yes, Miss Detective," he said, "that's mud from outside the pump house."—The Secret at Shadow Ranch

Nancy wears shoes that suit both her fashion style and her lifestyle. She dons sturdy brown low-heeled shoes when sleuthing, but goes for the gold when she's headed for a night out. As any sleuth knows, however, shoes lend themselves to more than mere accessory: **1** You can surmise someone's character by the shoes he wears; **2** you can tell a lot about a suspect by his footprints (see page 75); and **3** in an emergency, you can tap out coded messages with your heels (see page 124). Learning to read a person's shoes can help the amateur detective gain insight into someone's personality, attitude, and motives. For example, if a woman wears ballet flats, she tends to be down-to-earth, young at heart, and easy to get along with. But if she wears black, extremely sharp stilettos, she's more likely to be tough, calculating, and potentially dangerous. To judge a man by his shoes, check the following:

• **Loafers.** Slip-on loafers indicate a man who tends to be label-conscious and have lots of attitude, but not much

Loafers

Athletic Shoes

Flip-flops

Cowboy Boots

Bowling Shoes

Oxfords

sensitivity. He usually has a high-powered job, makes a lot of money—perhaps underhandedly—and likes to show it off.

- **Athletic Shoes.** Expensive athletic shoes are a sign of a man with plenty of disposable income who will show you a good time while stepping out on the town. He's probably an athlete, works in the sports field, and likes to have fun. But if the shoes are cheap sneakers, watch out: He may be a sneaky character.

- **Flip-flops.** Flip-flop guys are usually casual, relaxed, and unemployed. He's most likely tried some low-key jobs, such as newspaper delivery, sign-wearing, or fast-food service, but not for long. He makes his money discreetly buying and selling items (not always legally) on the streets, and slips out of his shoes to monkey-climb fences for a fast getaway.

- **Cowboy Boots.** Cowboy boots could mean a real cowboy or a poseur. He may work at an authentic dude ranch or a cheesy country-western bar. Look closely: Real cowboys wear scuffed and dusty boots that have seen the trails; poseurs' boots are all spit and polish.

- **Bowling Shoes.** A bowling shoe kind of guy is often whimsical, alternative, and unpredictable. He can be an interesting date. He probably works in the arts—songwriter, conceptual artist, poet—and is sensitive and creative, but cash poor. Then again, he could be a bowler.

- **Oxfords.** A guy in brown lace-up oxfords tends to be solid and down-to-earth. He believes in old-fashioned romance, marriage, and family and carries a ring around with him. It's a good bet he's not the criminal type (real criminals just don't wear oxfords).

Flirt and Use Your Feminine Wiles to Obtain Information

When the young sleuth told Tom Patrick about the furtive figure she had seen from the window, the officer grinned. She pointed to a window on the second floor. "That's my room. If you don't have a chance to use the door knocker, just throw a stone up against the screen to alert me." —The Hidden Staircase

Nancy does not need lessons on how to flirt. The girl detective seems to have a natural ability to gain the attention of attractive police officers, state troopers, young attorneys, wise professors, and other available men, often gathering important information in the process. If you tend to be shy, freeze up around men, or simply don't know how to flirt, here are some basics.

1 *Attract your target's attention.*

- Wear bright colors, bold lines, and geometric shapes that attract the eye.
- Make sure you're showing some skin.
- Accessorize with small but eye-catching adornments, such as an antique necklace, sparkly bracelet, dangling earrings, or jeweled wristwatch.
- Wear something special and unique, such as a diamond hair clip, silky scarf, or provocative pin.

2 Wear a scent that's light yet seductive.

Sexual attraction is highly chemical, thanks to hormones. Just don't overdo it with heavy scents. Men are turned off by cloying colognes and perfumes. A nice trick: Use a scented lotion all over your body instead of perfume.

3 Draw attention to your hair and face.

Fluffy hair, worn loose, is sexier than hair that's twisted up. Run your fingers through your tresses to call attention to those soft locks. Add a gardenia or ribbon to your coiffure for extra glamour. Next, accent your eyes, cheekbones, and lips with light but effective makeup. Then touch your face occasionally to pull his eyes in that direction.

4 Use nonverbal gestures.

- Smile, not just with your lips, but with your eyes. (Practice in front of a mirror to see the difference.)
- Accentuate your interest with frequent eyebrow lifts and flashing eyes. (But remember, no eye fluttering, which will make you seem deceitful.)
- Tilt your head while listening to him to show you're fascinated by him.
- Stand or sit with your arms open, not crossed.
- Lean in when he talks, as if you're hanging on every word.
- Nod frequently (but not excessively) to acknowledge him.

5 Let your eyes linger on his a little longer.

But be careful not to stare or glare at him, or zone out. You want to make eye contact last only a split second longer than necessary to let him know you're intrigued. The key is to be subtle and approachable.

6 *Use a cheerful voice when you speak.*

If you need an opening, "Hi, I'm (your name)" works well. So does introducing a topic related to the context, such as "Nice party," "Cool place," "Great food," etc. Give him plenty of compliments, but nothing too personal. Share something intimate about yourself when the time is right, but don't pour out all your problems. Tease him now and then to show you have a good sense of humor, but don't be sarcastic (it's a turn-off).

7 *Be a good listener.*

Nancy is a great detective because she knows how to get people to open up, even while she does most of the listening. Pay attention to your date, nod frequently, and say, "I know what you mean" or "Exactly!" Ask questions relevant to his remarks and repeat something he's said to let him know you understand.

8 *Encourage him to reveal his secrets.*

Smile, compliment him on how smart he is, and ask open-ended questions. Now that he's attracted to you, he'll lose sight of his goal to remain silent and ultimately spill the beans.

9 *Act as if you already know the information you want.*

Watch for signs that he may be lying: a lot of arm and hand movement, nervous fingers, higher-pitched voice, and lots of pauses in his speech.

Get the Most Out of Your Date

Although Nancy doesn't have a lot of time for dating with all the sleuthing she must do, she manages to take an occasional break and enjoy some fun in the company of a young suitor. When she does go to a party or dance, she makes the most of it, often combining dating and detecting. When a fellow is relaxed and under your spell, that's the best time to really get to know him, along with his dreams, his goals, and his deep, dark secrets.

1 Accept invitations from a variety of suitors.

You may be surprised to find that what you thought was your "type" may not be as interesting as a man who doesn't quite fit your mold. Like trying a range of foods or solving a number of mysteries, dating a variety of men makes life richer and helps you gain valuable experiences—and often information—from each encounter. Even a seemingly average guy can offer some surprises, if you know how to find them.

2 Take the time to dress up.

No matter whom you're dating or where you're going, this is the time to engage in a little dress-up fun. Pick out a new frock or enhance an older outfit with fresh accessories, such as a bold belt, a stunning necklace, or an antique brooch. If you're on a case, opt for a brooch that can pick a lock, a locket with a hidden microphone, or a necklace that doubles as a concealed camera. Then get a manicure with polish to match your outfit, and try a new alluring fragrance.

3 Look at the positive instead of the negative.

Sometimes a date goes well simply because you have a positive attitude. Even if he turns out to be a long-winded bore or self-serving egomaniac, think about what you're gaining from the experience: a new adventure, a nice dinner, an evening on the town, a chance to dress up—and perhaps a clue to a puzzling mystery.

4 Be your charming self.

We all have moods, even Nancy, although she tries her best to hide her negative ones. Dating is the perfect opportunity to be your witty and charming self. Bring up entertaining topics, such as a strange situation you've experienced while sleuthing or "hypothetical" mystery you're currently working on, to turn a dull date into an amusing—and revealing—evening.

5 Don't discuss past relationships.

This is not the time to talk about other men. Keep the focus on the two of you. If he asks about your previous boyfriends, simply say, "We weren't compatible." Don't blame the other party or drag out the details of the relationship. And don't ask him probing questions about his past relationships either. It's an obvious interrogation ploy that rarely produces useful information. If you want to uncover secrets, be subtle.

6 Determine your interest level in your date.

The first date offers the opportunity to get to know the other person as well as you can in a short period of time. Ask questions, listen attentively, and let him know when you agree with him. Don't be judgmental or make snap decisions about him early on—he may not be what he seems. Of course, you don't want to give him false hope if you're not interested in him, but don't discourage him first thing, either, or your plans for the date may be ruined.

7 Keep it light and fun.

Keep the conversation neutral. You may certainly discuss serious topics, such as a mystery investigation or curious clue you've discovered, but keep things positive; otherwise, he may think you have ulterior motives for the date. Draw him out on topics of interest, and if you're not familiar with something he says—such as an archaeological term, a canoeing maneuver, or a secret password—let him know. He'll enjoy telling you more.

Signs the date isn't working

- *He keeps looking at other women.*
- *He doesn't want dessert or after-dinner drinks.*
- *He answers his cell phone often.*
- *He goes to the bathroom more than once.*
- *He keeps checking his watch.*
- *He doesn't ask you any questions about yourself.*

Get That Ring on Your Finger and That Man to the Altar

Although Nancy is usually too busy to even think about getting married and settling down, she knows someday she'll be Mrs. Ned Nickerson. In the meantime, weddings are no mystery to Nancy, with all the bridal invitations she receives. Since many of her friends have tied the knot, she's gathered a few clues to catching a man and has some advice for those who are eager to walk down the aisle.

1 Hint at your intentions.

If you think your man is Mr. Right, and you've been together for some time, occasionally drop clues that you're interested in a lifetime commitment. Make them nonthreatening, such as, "We're great together, aren't we!" or "I love being with you," rather than nagging him to take the next step.

2 Remind him how much you have in common.

Sometimes a man needs to be reminded that he's got a good thing going and should make it permanent. Talk about how compatible you are, how well you get along, and how much you have in common. For example, you might say, "It's amazing that we both love raising carrier pigeons" or "We're so well matched at shuffleboard" or "I couldn't solve all these mysteries without your help."

3 Show him how much you care.

It's the little things that illustrate love and commitment to your partner, such as inviting him along on adventures, taking him boating, listening to his theories on a case, or rescuing him from quicksand. Be creative and show you care by slipping a note into his blazer pocket, knitting him a new sweater, or watching him score the winning point at football.

4 Set the stage for a romantic opportunity.

Give him the perfect opportunity to pop the question by arranging a candlelight dinner for two, a romantic weekend at the lake, or a lavish picnic in the park with champagne, watercress sandwiches, and Nancy's favorite, chocolate cake with walnut topping, for dessert. You can also set the mood

A champagne picnic in the park is the perfect
romantic scene for popping the question.

by taking a leisurely boat ride, cuddling up by the fire, or spending the night in a nearby inn. Just let him know what you have planned, and the ring should be forthcoming.

5 *Talk about your happily married friends.*

Occasionally reminisce about a friend's wedding and talk about how happy they seem now that they're married. Invite the loving couple to dinner to witness their wedded bliss. Ask the newlyweds to share their favorite things about being married. Afterward, discuss what impressed you about the couple and mention how similar they are to the two of you.

6 *Give him time.*

Don't hound him or give him an ultimatum—that will have the opposite effect. Keep your clues subtle, not overt, then stop talking about the subject for a while. Give him time to mull it over. Remember, you want him to feel it's his decision, even if he's following your lead.

Keep Romance Alive When You've Been Together Forever

Ned suddenly burst into laughter. "One thing that makes you so interesting, Nancy, is that I never know when I ask you to go out, what mystery will come our way!"—Sign of the Twisted Candles

It does seem as if Nancy Drew and Ned Nickerson have been together forever. Yet Nancy is able to keep Ned interested, even when she's busy solving a crime. He's fascinated by her independence, intelligence, and stick-to-itiveness, and he often joins in her mysterious adventures. More than once those adventures have been dangerous, even life threatening, but perhaps that's part of the appeal. Keeping romance alive over the years—and even decades—can be a challenge, but if anyone can be considered an expert in this area, it's Nancy Drew.

1 Surprise him.

Do something out of the ordinary once in a while to shake things up and catch him off guard. For example, you might send him a mysterious letter to decode or have chocolate chip cookies delivered to his dorm or office, just to say, "I'm thinking of you."

2 Do something he likes to do.

While many couples share a lot of interests, they often have their own separate activities as well. Enchant him by joining in one of his hobbies or activities from time to time. He'll appreciate the gesture.

3 Listen to him.

Sometimes we take our partner for granted and forget to really listen to him. If he's had a bad day at the university or office, pay attention by making eye contact, nodding in understanding, and adding your comments in support. You don't have to solve his problems, just allow him to express his emotions.

4 Plan a different kind of date.

If you're stuck in a rut, such as going to the same movie house or hanging out with the same friends, try something different. You might go to a séance, take a cruise to an exotic location, head for a dude ranch, or take in the circus. It can be anything, as long as it's new to the two of you.

5 Compliment your man.

Be specific. Remark on his looks and style sense ("Your eyes sparkle when you wear blue!"); or his recent accomplishments ("I'm so proud of your promotion!"); or his athleticism ("You really hit that ball out of the park!").

6 Remind him why he loves you.

Not overtly, of course, but in subtle ways. For example, if he loves your apple crisp, make it for him often. If he loves to hear your latest sleuthing triumphs, regale him with the clues in your current case. And if he loves to have you all to himself, spend a romantic, stay-in evening with him.

Help Your Sidekicks Kick-Start Their Love Lives

When it comes to offering love advice to her sidekicks, Nancy is a great resource. She knows how to attract and keep a man—she's done it for decades. She and her chums often discuss their relationships, not to mention their occasional crushes. If your sidekicks need a kick in the pants to get their love lives on track, try Nancy's advice.

 1 *Help her find a man.*

There are lots of ways to meet men. Invite your sidekick to frequent places where they hang out, and she's more likely to come in contact with attractive and available men. Consider the following venues:

- Pool hall, if she has some skill shooting pool
- Sporting event, such as football, baseball, ice hockey
- Beach, especially if she looks good in a bathing suit
- Athletic league, to join a co-ed sports team
- Laundromat, where single guys do their laundry
- Grocery store, at night or on weekends, when lonely guys go
- Dog park (if she doesn't have a dog, she can borrow one)
- Community event, such as a co-op garden night, band performance, or game night
- Gym, to get in shape and to find a man who's doing the same
- Bookstore, to share a love of reading

Encourage her to smile and be friendly.

Once your sidekick has her eye on a guy, remind her to smile even though she may be nervous. Give her a few tips on how to strike up a conversation, based on similar interests. For example, if she's at the grocery store, she might ask for advice on produce or meats. If she's at the dog park, she could remark on how smart his dog is.

Advise her to be open to a variety of men.

Your sidekick most likely has a list of traits she wants in a man. Have her reconsider her list and be open to other possibilities. Are her standards too high in terms of his looks, ambition, intelligence, sense of humor, and style? If so, explore other options. (Nancy would never judge a book by its cover.)

Suggest she learn from past mistakes.

It may be that your friend has had some bad experiences with men and is not as open to a relationship as she once was. Remind her that we've all been hurt at one time or another, but encourage her to move past this and not judge someone too soon. Everyone is unique, and everyone has something to offer.

Help her play up her best features.

If your sidekick is a little on the plump side, help her find clothes that make her look slimmer, give her some diet tips, and have her play up her good features, such as her blonde hair or sparkling eyes. If she's kind of tomboyish, help her find some flattering feminine outfits to bring out her softer side and suggest a new hairstyle or a little makeup.

6 *Remind her that love can surface anytime, anywhere.*

Your friend needs to be aware that love may be just around the corner. Remind her to be open and ready for any opportunity.

7 *Tell her to trust her instincts.*

As she gets to know a man, her heart may say one thing, but her gut may be telling her something is amiss. Encourage her to watch for red flags, such as excessive drinking or making nasty comments to the help. If she's too anxious about getting a man, she may lose her perspective, so you'll need to step in if you see a potential problem.

8 *Give her advice as needed.*

If she needs tips on flirting or a makeover, offer her suggestions. If she's dating a married man, let her know this is a bad idea. If you suspect the man has a dark past, do a little investigating to find out about skeletons in his closet. Then let her know (gently) what you've discovered.

CHAPTER **5**

*Escape
Clues*

HOW TO

Thwart a Kidnapping

Nancy has been kidnapped a number of times, and so have her friends and acquaintances. (Even Carson Drew has been the victim of kidnappers.) When she finds herself bound with rope in the back of a thug's car, Nancy tries to remain calm, knowing that keeping her head will help her out of this jam. Most kidnapping victims are released quickly and unharmed. But kidnappings are serious crimes. Here are some ways to avoid being abducted and steps to take if you are.

1 Be alert at all times.

Trust your instincts. Always be alert to your surroundings, especially when investigating a place with which you're not familiar or where the criminal element is in evidence.

- Get your car keys out on your way to your roadster, then lock the doors immediately once you're inside.
- Avoid dark alleyways, deserted cabins, and suspicious mansions.
- Be aware of who's around you, where you could escape to if accosted, and what weapon you could use if assaulted.
- Carry a cell phone, whistle, flashlight, mace, and pepper spray everywhere you go.

2 If you are accosted, call the police.

If you have a cell phone, dial the police emergency number.

If you act quickly, the police will have the chance to rescue you before the kidnappers get too far. If you can't use your phone immediately, conceal it so you can use it later, when you're left alone. If you have no access to a phone, try to leave a written or coded message.

❸ Scream loudly and make a scene.

Screaming may be enough to scare the kidnapper away. It will also alert others nearby to come to your rescue or call the police. Most kidnappers want to remain inconspicuous, so this kind of attention will encourage them to disappear. Instead of yelling "Help!" which is often ignored, yell "I'm being kidnapped!" or "Fire!" to gain attention.

❹ Fight tooth and nail to defend yourself.

You can use your body as a weapon, to block an attack or go on the offensive.

- Instead of punching the assailant's face with your fist, which is like hitting a brick wall, open your palm and slap, scratch, and grab at the kidnapper's face.
- Pry away his grabbing hands with your fingers.
- Jab your elbows or knees into the attacker's body, especially his groin.

- Find something with which to poke, gouge, scratch, or wound the kidnapper, such as a pen, flashlight, hair clip, handbag, or cell phone.
- Aim for the eyes and throat. Become a human windmill and thrash the heck out of him with your wildly flailing arms and legs.

5 *Try to escape.*

As soon as you get the opportunity, run. If your attacker wants your handbag or money, throw it at him and use this distraction to help you get away. Be careful not to run into oncoming traffic, or put yourself in harm's way. But don't hesitate to take the chance to escape.

6 *If your attempt fails, do not antagonize your captors.*

Criminals are usually stupid. Although they think they've planned every last detail, things go wrong, and their mistakes will give you the opportunity to escape. Take stock of the situation. Act cooperatively while looking for ways to slip away. Try to ascertain why you've been kidnapped so you know how to negotiate with your attackers. Remember, most kidnappers want you alive for a reason.

7 *Be observant while in captivity.*

Stay calm and study your attacker. Memorize details about him to share with the police when you're freed. Remember things such as physical marks or scars, clothing, height and weight, voice, facial details, smell, and so on, as well as details about your surroundings.

8 *Cooperate with your captor to gain his trust.*

Instead of making threats or being hostile, cooperate. Don't beg or become hysterical, but let him know that you're a person, you have family that cares for you, you have dreams and ambitions. Try to find something in common to help him bond with you and create empathy. Be a good listener as you determine the psychology of your captor.

9 *Take your next opportunity to escape.*

The next time you ascertain that help may be nearby (either your captor has you on the move or there are visitors to your hideout), feign a fainting spell or illness. While your captor is distracted, determine the best way to alert bystanders to your presence (write a note or communicate in code to anyone who may be nearby).

10 *Seek help once you've escaped.*

Once you've managed to escape your captors, run to the nearest store, residence, or police station and report the details. Tell your rescuers that you've just escaped a kidnapping and that your family and friends are searching for you. Mention that a possible reward may be involved.

Write SOS
Backward with Lipstick

The young sleuth suddenly remembered the lipstick she was carrying in her skirt pocket. She twisted the end until the red stick was showing. With the lipstick, she wrote a large SOS backwards on the pane so that it would be legible from the outside. —The Mystery of the Fire Dragon

Nancy has practiced sending all kind of messages, codes, and signals when she's in danger. Even if she's tied up with rope and being held captive on an airplane, she'll manage to find her lipstick and write a message on the window-pane. In the event that you find yourself in similar trouble, here are some tips for communicating your situation to others using nothing more than a simple tube of lipstick.

1 Carry a red or dark-colored lipstick at all times.

While most women pack along a lipstick to refresh their lips throughout the day, few realize that lipstick can save their lives. Nancy carries a red lipstick that's easily spotted from a distance and can be used to write large letters on a win-dowpane, wall, or other surface.

2 Practice writing backward before your next mystery.

Lipsticks can be expensive, so when you're practicing back-ward writing, use an inexpensive red marker. To learn how to write in reverse, write the alphabet, then hold it up to a mirror and copy down what you see. Practice writing the letters in their mirrored form until your script is smooth and the letters feel natural.

3 *Locate a window visible to the outside.*

If you find yourself held captive on an airplane, in an automobile, or inside a hidden attic room, locate a window that can be seen by passersby.

4 *Extricate your lipstick.*

If you're tied up, wiggle and squirm around to loosen your rope bonds (see "How to Escape from Rope Bonds," page 128). Then retrieve your lipstick from your pocket or nearby handbag.

5 *Remove the cap and unroll the lipstick.*

Once you have the lipstick, be careful not to drop it. Ease off the cap with your fingertips, then carefully unroll the stick about halfway (to prevent it from breaking off).

6 *Write SOS on the windowpane.*

Write the letters "SOS" backward, as large as you can, so passersby can read the message from afar.

Escape from a Locked Room

In general, before you set out on a potentially danger-ous mission, it's wise to leave an easy-to-find note that describes where you're going so your pals can find you. Be as specific as you can, with a map showing where you're going and how to get there, the time you left, and any dangers they may encounter along the way. When you find yourself trapped, follow the steps below.

1 *Don't panic.*

You'll think of something if you keep your wits about you. If you panic, you'll just make things worse.

2 *Yell for help.*

Scream your lungs out. More than likely there's someone nearby who will hear your shrieks and come to your rescue.

3 *Pound on the walls.*

The walls may be old and crumbling and eventually collapse under your force, freeing you. If nothing else, the pounding may attract the attention of others in the vicinity.

4 *Tap SOS with the heel of your shoe.*

Tap three quick taps, then three slow taps, then another three quick taps. Everyone knows what SOS means: Help! If you don't have a good solid heel, rap with your flashlight, cell phone, a rock, or your knuckles. (See "How to Tap Out a Morse Code Message with Your High-Heeled Shoes," page 124.)

⑤ Search your surroundings for a tool to help you escape.

Look around for a chisel, crowbar, or tire iron. Most attics, dungeons, and towers have items lying around that can be used to pry or break open a door or window.

⑥ Use items in your trusty handbag.

Use a nail file, eyebrow tweezers, skeleton key, or other object from your purse or cosmetic case to jimmy the lock. (See "How to Pack the Perfect Handbag for All Contingencies," page 28.)

⑦ If all else fails, wait for your friends to rescue you.

Remember that note you left for your sidekicks (or fiancé)? Simply wait for your friends (or young man) to follow your trail. You can always count on them to show up in the nick of time.

Tap Out a Morse Code Message with Your High-Heeled Shoes

Nancy had noticed that the tapping sounds were uneven. It occurred to her that possibly they were a code. She could not translate any of the tapping sounds into words, but on a hunch she tapped out in Morse code: "Who are you?"—The Clue of the Tapping Heels

During an especially puzzling mystery, Nancy recognized a staccato tapping noise as a Morse-coded message and was able to tap back an important coded response. If you find yourself unable to communicate in the typical ways—perhaps you've been gagged and bound—consider tapping out a message in Morse code with your high-heeled shoes.

❶ Study Morse code.

Learning the code isn't difficult if you concentrate on how each letter sounds. A dash is a long tap and a dot is a shorter, staccato tap, but you need to listen to the letter as a whole, not as mere dots and dashes. For example, "a" would be pronounced "dit-dah" rather than "dot-dash."

❷ Practice with your sidekicks.

Once you've learned the Morse code alphabet, practice sending messages back and forth with your sidekicks.

A	. -	N	- .
B	- . . .	O	- - -
C	- . - .	P	. - - .
D	- . .	Q	- - . -
E	.	R	. - .
F	. . - .	S	. . .
G	- - .	T	-
H	. . . .	U	. . -
I	. .	V	. . . -
J	. - - -	W	. - -
K	- . -	X	- . . -
L	. - . .	Y	- . - -
M	- -	Z	- - . .

- Stiletto heels are perfect for tapping precision, but oxfords with at least a two-inch heel will work well for your purpose.
- If you're right-foot dominant, use the edge of your right heel to tap the code. (Use your left foot if you're left-foot dominant.)
- Spend an hour each day to increase your speed, and soon you'll be able to communicate rapidly. Once you have the hang of things, have one of your friends "receive" your message in a room next door or a floor above or below you.

3 *Try to distinguish between random taps and coded taps.*

When investigating mysterious tapping sounds, listen carefully to determine whether it's a coded message or just random tapping. While the noise may be coming from a suspicious character searching for something in the house, it may also just be a branch rhythmically hitting a window-pane or a small animal gnawing through flooring, roofing, and the like. (Codes are repeated exactly, while random taps are unlikely to be as precisely repetitive.)

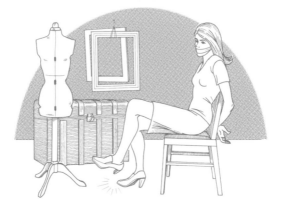

Morse code messages can alert others that you are in need of immediate help.

4 Respond to the taps in kind.

If you do recognize the sounds as Morse code, reply to the message by tapping out a response with your heel.

5 If you're not wearing heels, improvise.

You can also use a hammer, silverware, or your knuckles to tap out a code.

Tapping for Help

When Nancy was tied up and gagged in an attic while investigating a mystery, she managed to inch her way to the door, face downward on the floor, and tap her heels loudly on the attic door to relay a coded cry for help. If you find yourself bound and gagged, or otherwise incapacitated, use Morse code to alert your rescuers:

* Determine the surface that will best conduct your tapping: the wall, the floor, or the door of the room in which you're held captive.
* Try to position your feet in close proximity to the wall, floor, or door.
* Get sufficient leverage so that you can tap with enough force to make your presence known.
* You may become exhausted tapping furiously, but don't give up. Rest for a few minutes, then begin again, with more force than before. Someone is bound to hear you and come to your rescue.

Escape from Rope Bonds

Nancy has been bound in ropes more times than she can count, but she manages to escape with a little ingenuity. If you find yourself all tied up in knots, try the following tips to free yourself.

1 Take a deep breath.

As you're being tied up, inhale deeply so that when you exhale, the rope will offer some slack. Do this subtly so your captors are not aware that you are planning to escape.

2 Wriggle your wrists against the ropes.

When your captors leave you alone, try to wriggle against your bonds where they're secured (typically at the wrist). This will help you find any loose or slack areas in the rope. Maintaining pressure and wriggling against the loose section may be enough to free you immediately or at least sufficiently to get your hands loose to untie the rest.

3 Remove shoes or clothing.

Kick off your shoes. This will allow your feet to work on the ropes and gain some slack in the bonds. If you're wearing a coat or other thick clothing and can wriggle out of it, this will also cause the rope to slacken, which may allow you to gain your freedom.

4 *Check for tools to cut the rope.*

Use items from your purse—such as a nail file or nail scissors—to weaken or cut the rope. If you can't reach your purse, look around for an object in the room that could cut the rope, such as a table corner or a sharp piece of equipment or tool.

5 *Chew the rope.*

If you can't find anything else to cut the rope, use your teeth. Chew at the strands a little bit at a time, until each one breaks free.

6 *Free yourself from the object you are secured to.*

Sometimes you can uproot the object you're bound to more easily than you can cut the rope. Try standing with the chair you're tied to, then attempt to break the chair's legs against the floor or a nearby wall. Slip your bonds free of the chair.

Avoid Being Drugged

A girl sleuth can't be too careful these days, especially when it comes to being drugged. Nancy has found herself befogged on more than one occasion. There are some easy ways to avoid this dangerous situation and to protect yourself from bad men who want to kidnap you for ransom or sleazy guys who have nefarious intentions.

1 *Always be alert to your environment.*

If you're out at a party, bar, or social club, never leave your drink unattended while you head for the dance floor or the ladies' room. Keep an eye out for suspicious types who seem to be watching you, and avoid them.

2 *Don't accept free drinks.*

Never accept drinks from strangers; they may be contaminated with sleeping powders or other drugs. Order your own drinks and make sure they come from a reputable bartender with a license in Mixology. If you're younger than twenty-one years old, limit yourself to sodas, power drinks, and virgin Chocolate Martinis.

3 *Use the buddy system.*

Whenever possible, have your sidekicks watch out for you, and do the same for them. If you see someone hovering around your friends' drinks with a bottle of unidentified pills or a vial of suspicious liquid, arrange to "accidentally" spill the drink.

4 *Be alert to the signs of drug ingestion.*

Check for the following signs:

- Impaired judgment (offering to pay the tab)
- Disinhibition (showing more than a little cleavage)
- Dizziness (falling off the barstool)
- Confusion (not being able to tell George from Bess, or George from Ned)
- Drowsiness (falling asleep in the middle of a stakeout)
- Uncoordinated movement (unable to stand and perform karaoke at the same time)

5 *If you think you've been drugged, take quick action.*

If you find you can no longer think clearly or communicate with others, or if you sense danger, you could be under the influence of a powerful and dangerous drug. Take immediate steps.

- Call emergency services and tell them you suspect you've been drugged.
- Seek medical attention. Let them know what drug you may have been given, or bring the container with you.
- Drink water to help dilute the drug.
- Have a friend tend to you while you await an ambulance or medical care.
- Try to stay awake by pinching yourself, walking with the assistance of a friend, or seeking cold air.

Two dangerous drugs a girl sleuth must avoid at all costs

- Sodium Pentothal. Also known as Truth Serum, this treacherous drug is used to obtain information from an unwilling subject. Signs you've been drugged with sodium pentothal include talking too much and spilling all your innermost secrets. Seek medical attention at once.

- Curare. This bitter tropical plant, easily disguised in a Mai Tai or fired through a blowgun, is often used to turn innocent people into zombies. Signs you've been drugged with curare include relaxed muscles, slowed breathing, and paralysis, all of which will require immediate medical attention.

Survive Hypnosis

Nancy has solved many cases involving hypnosis and has had to contend with people who are in trancelike states. She's even experienced it herself. It is believed that when under a hypnotic state, a person becomes extremely relaxed and suggestible and will respond to the hypnotist's commands. If asked, she may hold up an arm, cluck like a chicken, and even do evil bidding. This couldn't be further from the truth. The subject has to be willing for the hypnotic state to be induced. And you cannot be hypnotized if you resist.

1 Understand the different methods of hypnosis.

There are three main methods used to hypnotize a subject:

- **Fixed gaze.** This old-fashioned method requires the subject to focus on the hypnotist's watch or other eye-catching object while listening to him speak in a low, monotone voice. This supposedly lulls the subject to "sleep."

- **Rapid.** In this method, the hypnotist bombards the subject with forceful commands, causing her to respond without thinking. This is usually performed on a stage in Las Vegas, in front of a large, intoxicated audience.

- **Progressive relaxation and imagery.** This is the method used by most psychiatrists. The hypnotist slowly brings the subject to a relaxed state, making her susceptible to post-hypnotic suggestions, such as, "You will quit smoking and eating so much."

2 Determine your susceptibility.

Basically, only susceptible subjects can be transformed into zombielike states. Ask yourself these questions: Are you the type of person who can relax in front of millions of people? Do you have a strong desire to be cast under a spell? If not, you're most likely not susceptible. And even if you are a little susceptible, the depth of hypnosis varies from person to person, ranging anywhere from a light stupor to a deep trance.

3 Recognize the signs that you're being hypnotized.

If someone asks you to relax and close your eyes while he speaks in a soft, monotone voice, he may be trying to hypnotize you. He may ask you to take deep breaths, forget about your problems, and release your tense muscles. He may then suggest you imagine a serene scene, repeating imagery, as he takes you deeper into the trance. Or he may have you stare at a small object on a blank wall while asking you to listen to his words.

4 Resist.

If you find yourself beginning to relax while listening to a hypnotic voice, think of something to occupy your mind, like counting to a hundred by fives, reciting a memorized poem, working on a mental puzzle, or trying to solve your current mystery. Drinking a triple latte may help, unless caffeine causes you to relax. Also be aware of any distractions in the room—a ticking clock, a bird outside the window.

Focusing mentally on one of these will help keep you from falling under a spell.

5 *If you fall into a trance, remember you are still in control.*

Signs that you have fallen into a trance include rapid eye movement and heavy breathing, as if you're asleep. But remember, if you should fall into a trance, you will not do anything under hypnosis that you wouldn't normally do. (For example, you won't hurt someone unless you really want to.)

6 *Snap out of it.*

Have a friend count to ten to bring you out of the spell slowly, rather than abruptly, which could cause temporary memory loss and startle you. If that doesn't work, have them nudge or pinch you to awaken you from the deep sleep.

7 *Be alert to signs of post-hypnotic suggestion.*

If you've been under a hypnotic trance, the hypnotist may have induced a post-hypnotic suggestion (PHS). For example, he may suggest that you think differently about something, such as pursuing criminals, or that you believe something, such as that you have more self-confidence. The power of the suggestion wears off quickly if the subject's core belief does not agree with the suggestion. If you have strong beliefs, these won't be changed by a PHS.

Outfit Your Car for Emergencies

Nancy almost never goes anywhere unprepared—or without the proper tools and equipment. Since she motors a lot, she keeps most of her sleuthing equipment in her car in case she needs to solve a crime, investigate a mystery, or handle an emergency. Follow Nancy's lead and make sure your car's glove compartment and trunk are properly outfitted.

1 Think safety first.

Take a course in mechanics to learn possible sources of automobile problems. Include a set of booster cables, tire chains, spare tire, and emergency road service information in the trunk. Tuck an extra flashlight in the glove compartment in case the one in your handbag dies. And always carry or hide an extra key in case you're locked out of the car.

2 Keep the car safe from theft.

Most cars are stolen for their parts. Keep yours safe from theft by rolling up the windows, putting up the convertible top, and locking all the doors each time you leave your car. Invest in some antitheft devices, such as an auto alarm system that activates the horn or a siren that's triggered by motion, sound, or contact. You can also buy a brake and steering wheel lock to immobilize the controls, hide a transmitter in the car so law enforcement can track it, and put a

sticker on the window warning thieves that your car is pro-
tected. But the best way to prevent car theft is simply not
leaving your keys in the vehicle. Other tips include:

- Keep valuables out of sight.
- Don't hide spare keys in obvious places.
- Park in well-lit areas.
- Never leave the car running unattended.

❸ *Have essentials on hand for emergencies.*

Your roadster is the perfect place to store items for emergencies. You never know when you'll find your tires slashed,
the weather changed, or other dire situations while you're
out and about. Here's a basic list of emergency equipment
to have on hand:

- Flashlights, with extra batteries, in case the lights go out
  or you need to explore a dark mansion
- First-aid kit, in case someone is bitten by a poisonous
  snake or vicious dog
- Pocket knife, to cut through rope bonds
- Blankets or sleeping bags in case you need to spend the
  night investigating a haunting
- Non-perishable food, for long stake-outs
- Candle and waterproof matches in case the flashlights
  don't work

❹ *Pack additional supplies for the long haul.*

Once you've packed the necessities, think about other items
you might need during your travels:

- Small tool set, including pliers, wrench, screwdriver, hammer
- Plastic boots and raincoat with hood

- Mittens, socks, and wool cap
- Overnight bag containing pajamas and robe, two changes of clothing, toilet articles, and a bathing suit, for disguise or last-minute plans
- Small collapsible shovel to use as a weapon, dig out of a snowstorm, or dig up clues

Emergency essentials every detective should store in her car trunk and glove compartment.

Escape from a Locked Car Trunk

Nancy has managed to rescue a victim who was trapped in the trunk of a car, but others haven't been so lucky. More than three hundred people nationwide have died from trunk entrapment in the past thirty years, and many more have been hospitalized. Many trunks are airtight, so suffocation is usually the cause of death. If you're ever forced into a trunk by a ruthless criminal, or you accidentally find yourself trapped, follow the steps below.

1 Remain calm.

If you panic, you may hyperventilate, which affects your thought processes and could impair your ability to free yourself. Stay calm, breathe slowly, and try to relax.

2 Search for a trunk release.

If you own a new model roadster, chances are it has a trunk release. Check the trunk area carefully for a metal handle, cord, button, or toggle switch near the trunk latch. If you can't find one, try feeling for a cable trunk release underneath the carpet on the driver's side, and yank it hard to release the trunk. If you own an older model car, consider buying a trunk release kit. They're inexpensive and can be professionally installed if you're not mechanically inclined. Choose one that comes with a remote, then keep a spare handy.

3 Access emergency tools in the trunk or glove compartment.

When outfitting your car, you should make sure you have a crowbar, tire iron, and screwdriver in the trunk and an extra screwdriver in your glove compartment, in case you need to free yourself or someone else who's locked in a trunk. If you're trapped inside, use the crowbar or screwdriver to pry open the latch—or to attract attention from passersby by pounding on the trunk lid. Insert the tool in the gap near the trunk latch and pry it up like a large can opener. If you can't unlock the trunk, at least you'll let in air and may be able to signal for help.

4 Try to escape through the back seat.

If the back seat of the car folds down to allow access to the trunk, you may be able to escape this way. Look for a release by inserting your fingers through the seat or around the side of the seat. The release may even be located in the trunk itself. If you can't find a release, push, kick, or pry the seat down to free yourself.

5 Push out the brake lights.

If you can access the brake lights from inside the trunk, pull or pry off the panel that covers them, then rip out the wires. Once the area is clear, push or kick the lights all the way through. Stick your hand out of the opening to signal to passersby for help or call for help through the hole. If nothing else, the police may stop the car for a broken taillight, which will lead to your rescue.

Get Your Car out of a Ditch

Even though Nancy is a cautious driver and rarely goes over the speed limit, she has found herself in a ditch on more than one occasion, often when being chased by a villain. Driving under stressful conditions may cause you to slip off the road or have an accident. Here are some tips to remember if your roadster is forced off the road and you find yourself stuck in a ditch.

1 Stay calm.

If your car starts to slide off the road and into a ditch, don't panic. That will only cause you to slam on your brakes and send you skidding across the pavement. Keep your head, and you'll have better control over your car.

2 Ease up on the accelerator.

If you try to accelerate out of the ditch, go easy on the gas pedal. Otherwise, you may cause the wheels to lose traction and spin in place. Shift the car into second gear for better traction on a slippery surface.

3 Force an object under the wheel for traction.

Place a length of burlap or other cloth, or a slat of wood or cardboard, as far under the tires as possible to give the wheels something to grip.

4 *Sprinkle sand or other gritty substance under your tires.*

This should provide some traction to help you free the car.

5 *If you are still unable to free your car, wave down a passerby.*

Turn on your flashers, hang a scarf on the antenna, or raise the hood to attract attention. Just make sure you don't wave down any criminals who may be pursuing you.

6 *Rock the car gently to gain momentum.*

Direct your good Samaritan to a position at the back of the car while you take the wheel. Have him or her push on the car to rock it back and forth and roll the car out of the ditch.

7 *Do not leave the car unless you know where you are.*

If you don't know for sure that help is close by, and you can't see anyone beyond one hundred yards, stay in your car. You may become disoriented or lost if you abandon your vehicle in an unfamiliar area. If it's cold, run the engine and heater ten minutes each hour.

8 *Wait for help to arrive.*

If you're stuck and can't move your car, don't panic. Help will arrive eventually, as long as someone knows approximately where you are. If your cell phone is working, call the auto club or a tow truck. They'll come to your rescue as soon as they can.

Survive When Your Car's Brakes Are Cut

Although Nancy usually keeps a cool head, she knows the seriousness of an out-of-control car. One of the causes is failed brakes, brought on by a number of reasons—they get wet in a storm, they haven't been properly cared for, they're faulty, or someone has cut them. If the unimaginable happens to you, follow these simple steps to safety.

1 *Remain calm.*

Having your breaks go out is an extremely scary and dangerous situation, but it is manageable. Keep your wits about you, and you'll be able to bring your roadster to a safe, albeit bumpy halt.

2 *Take your foot off the gas.*

Obviously, you don't want to accelerate when your brakes go out, so remove your foot from the gas pedal immediately. If you have cruise control, turn it off.

3 *Pump your brakes.*

Instead of jamming on the brakes and pressing them down to the floor, pump your brakes rapidly. Although it may take several attempts, this should rebuild enough pressure in the braking system to stop the car.

4 Downshift into low gear.

If your roadster is a stick shift, downshift, moving into each lower gear until you're in the lowest gear possible. If you have an automatic transmission, shift into low or "L."

5 Use the emergency brake.

The emergency or parking brake can usually stop a vehicle, although it will take longer. Slowly and steadily pull the handle or push down on the pedal, depending on the type of emergency brake you have. Do not engage the brake quickly, or you may lose control of your vehicle.

6 Keep your eyes on the road.

Don't lose track of the road ahead. Continue to steer the car, alert to obstacles ahead of you. Carefully maneuver around traffic, large objects, and pedestrians.

7 Warn other drivers and pedestrians.

Alert others in the vicinity that you're having car problems. Turn on your hazard lights, honk your horn, and yell/wave out the window so drivers and pedestrians stay out of the way.

8 Slow the vehicle however you can.

If the car is still moving, look for a gradual incline, ramp, or street. Don't make any sudden swerves or you may overturn the vehicle. Instead, use the hill to slow down the vehicle. Find an open space where you can allow the car to come to a stop. Or drive through gravel, dirt, grass, or small shrubbery to slow your car. Just be careful of large trees—they can be fatal.

CHAPTER 6

Survival Clues

Fend Off a Poisonous Snake and Treat Snakebite

Nancy knelt on one knee, pulled off the lid, then shrieked in terror! The box contained a large copper-colored snake! Disturbed, it reared and the head darted toward Nancy, fangs out.—The Clue of the Twisted Candles

Nancy has come close to being bitten by a snake several times. She's been lucky. Each year, approximately seven thousand people receive bites from poisonous snakes in the United States alone. Even a bite from a so-called harmless snake can cause infection or allergic reaction. Those who frequent wilderness areas, or camp, hike, picnic or live in snake-inhabited areas—or investigate mysteries in unfamiliar places—should be aware of the potential dangers posed by venomous snakes.

1 Use caution, particularly in snake country.

Never put your hands in dark places such as rock crevices, heavy brush, hollow logs, or mysterious boxes without first making sure they are safe. If you're headed for snake country, prepare ahead of time by bringing along a snakebite kit and be sure you know how to use it.

2 Assume that any snake you see is potentially poisonous.

It's not easy distinguishing between poisonous and nonpoisonous snakes. The only difference is the presence of poison fangs and glands, which you cannot determine at a glance. Only about 5 percent, or roughly twenty-five species, of snakes in the United States are poisonous. The most common poisonous snakebites are caused by pit vipers—rattlesnakes, copperheads, and cottonmouth (water moccasin) snakes—and coral snakes. Most snakes avoid people, but some will attack on occasion.

3 *When you come face to face with a snake, avoid contact.*

Do not try to handle a snake or kill it unless you have special training. Back off slowly; the snake senses your body heat and movement. If he is about to strike, use a shovel, garden rake, or stick to fend off the attack.

4 *If bitten, check for symptoms of a poisonous bite.*

Look for the following signs:

- Fang marks in the skin, discoloration and swelling at the site
- Bloody discharge from the wound
- Severe localized pain, burning fever, enlarged lymph nodes near area
- Diarrhea, nausea, vomiting, sweating, increased thirst
- Breathing difficulties, dizziness, weakness, blurred vision, numbness, tingling
- Fainting, loss of muscle coordination, rapid pulse, convulsions, shock, paralysis
- Altered mental state

Call for immediate medical assistance, then follow the steps for "Treating a Snakebite" (page 148).

Treating a Snakebite

While waiting for help to arrive:
- *Keep the bitten area lower than the heart.*
- *Remove jewelry and clothing that may restrict blood flow and swelling.*
- *Wash the bite with soap and water or antiseptic solution.*
- *Cover the area with a cool compress to minimize swelling and pain.*
- *Monitor breathing and heart rate.*

If help hasn't arrived within 30 minutes:
- *Wrap a bandage two to four inches above the bite to slow the venom. Do not apply a tourniquet, which cuts off the flow of blood.*
- *Place a suction device over the bite to help draw venom out of the wound. Do not make an incision.*
- *Make every effort to get medical assistance.*

Note Tourniquets, incisions, and using your mouth to suck out the venom are treatments no longer considered effective.

When medical help arrives:
- *Identify or describe the snake that bit the victim so they can use the correct antivenin (antidote to snake venom).*
- *Stay out of the way while the victim is treated and taken to a nearby hospital.*

Avoid an Alligator Attack

When exploring or investigating unfamiliar places, such as the swamps in Florida, you'll need to be especially alert to danger at all times. One of the most frightening experiences you may meet is a surprise attack by an alligator. Here are ways to avoid a lethal encounter.

1 Understand the risk of attack.

Alligators rely on very basic instincts that are geared mainly for procuring food. For this oversized lizard, you could be on the menu. He'll eat whatever he can to maintain his 600-pound weight—including you.

2 Know their habits.

Alligators usually sleep during the day and feed at night, so be especially cautious if you're exploring the swamps after dark. Gators are difficult to see then, except for their red, glowing eyes. But by the time you see their eyes, it may be too late. Avoid swimming at dusk, night, or dawn; that's feeding time.

3 Stay away from the water.

If possible, keep your investigation on dry land and avoid the water's edge, where gators tend to hide in the reeds. Alligators are fresh-water reptiles, but they've been spotted in the ocean on occasion. If you plan to swim, make sure it's only in clear water where there are no grasses nearby.

4 *Keep alert.*

Always scan the area in search of movement or other signs of something lurking. If you spot an alligator, get out of the water at once and move as far away as possible.

Skin Dive

Nancy's skill in skin and scuba diving has served her well in a couple of adventures. She's had to search for clues underwater—and even rescue another diver. Skin diving, also known as free diving, is the sport of swimming underwater with a face mask and flippers but without portable oxygen equipment, such as a scuba tank. Skin diving is an exciting sport, but it can also be dangerous if you're not trained and lack the confidence to do it. Here are some tips to get you started in skin diving, should your sleuthing require some underwater exploration.

1 Make sure you're in good health.

Nancy is in perfect health, so she has no problems holding her breath for long periods, moving about in the water, or diving down deep. Don't dive if you have health problems, such as heart disease, or breathing difficulties. Get a checkup before you go diving to ensure your safety.

2 Take a course in skin diving.

You'll find courses offered at a local college, recreation center, YMCA, or private swim and diving schools. Make sure your instructor is certified and belongs to a recognized organization, such as the National Association of Underwater Instructors, before you enroll in a class.

3 Find a buddy.

Always bring along a buddy who is also trained in diving, so you can help each other if one's foot becomes wedged between two rocks or you experience other mishaps. Before your dive, establish a plan in case of emergency. Never be more than a few feet apart from your buddy.

4 Get the proper equipment.

Buy or rent the following items:
- Bathing suit, preferably stylish and attractive
- Mask, tempered for pressure, with a nose enclosure
- Large fins with a strap around the back
- Snorkel with a purge valve
- Neoprene gloves and booties, for protection against cold water, rough surfaces, or stings from ocean creatures
- Rubber insulation suit, wet suit, or dry suit with a removable hood

Nice to have:
- Diving knife in case of emergency
- Underwater writing slate if you don't know sign language
- Compass to keep track of your direction
- Diving light to see in dark areas
- Underwater camera to take pictures of sea life

5 Practice holding your breath.

You can increase your breath-holding capacity through practice. This enables you to dive under the surface for longer periods. But don't overestimate your abilities or you could end up in real danger.

6 *Learn diver's sign language.*

Most of the signs are based on ASL—American Sign Language—but some are unique to divers. As long as you and your buddy know the signs you're using, you'll be able to communicate underwater. Here are some basic signs used by divers.

- "OK": Make a circle by connecting your thumb and index finger.
- "Going down": Turn your thumb down.

Communication is critical when skin diving, particularly when danger lurks.

- "Going up": Turn your thumb up.
- "Go that way": Point with your index finger.
- "Stay there": Hold up your hand, palm out, like a stop signal.
- "Come here": Wave toward yourself.
- "Under/over/around": Move your hand under, over, or around an imaginary object.
- "Watch me": Point to your chest.
- "Look at that": Point to your goggles with your index and middle finger, then to the object.
- "Danger!": Make a fist, hold it out to the side, and move it up and down like you're pounding a table.
- "Help!": At the surface, wave your hand to alert the boat crew you need help.

7 *Find a safe place to dive.*

The local dive shop is a great source for good, safe diving spots. Don't dive in bad weather, at night, or when currents are strong. Currents become significantly stronger as you dive farther down, so be cautious when diving below twenty feet. (Also, be wary of spears that may come hurtling from behind big rocks while you're investigating a mystery.)

8 *If you're caught in a strong current, don't panic.*

Swim parallel to the shore until you can pull away from the grip of the current. If an emergency arises, know how to drift dive—go with the flow until the current lessens in strength.

Paddle a Canoe—and Save Yourself If You Spring a Leak

Nancy is an able sailor and expert boater, and she even knows a thing or two about canoeing, which can be tricky for the inexperienced. Forward paddling, a seemingly simple task, can take months to learn. If you're intrepid, like Nancy, that won't stop you from learning how to master the skill of canoeing. It may come in handy as a way to help you search for a phantom launch—or as your only means of escape.

1 Prepare for canoeing.

Always wear a life vest and be sure to take a basic canoeing course from a professional before setting out on your own. Make sure the canoe is in good condition and that there are no apparent leaks, which could sink your canoe in the middle of the lake.

2 Board the canoe.

Carefully step into the canoe, placing one foot in the center. Grasp the sides of the canoe and lift the other foot in. Kneel or sit near the stern or bow if there is another person in the boat. If you're alone, stick to the middle. Make sure the canoe is balanced and the load is distributed evenly to avoid tipping it over. Place the heaviest part of the load in the center. You don't want to overload the canoe, but a boat that's too light is also likely to overturn.

3 Grip the paddle.

Grasp the top of the paddle with the inside hand, and with the hand closer to the water, hold the paddle at a comfortable point, about two to three feet down. Hold it about two feet in front of you and dip the blade into the water. While you pull your bottom hand back, push your top hand forward, keeping the paddle at chest level.

Paddle furiously to propel the canoe forward when you're in hot pursuit.

4 *Propel the canoe forward.*

If you're in hot pursuit of a suspect or a clue, paddle furiously. The canoe will glide forward at racing speed.

When Your Canoe Leaks

Just when you have the solution to the mystery within your grasp, you may find you've sprung a leak. This is often due to sabotage intended to waylay you from pursuing your quest. If this happens:

- *Find the source of the leak and fill it with newspaper, a piece of your clothing, or other object to stop the influx of water.*
- *Bail excess water out of the canoe with a cup, can, or bottle.*
- *If the canoe has a serious leak, get to the side of the river and step out into shallow water.*
- *If you have no chance of saving the canoe and have to abandon ship, grab the paddle and swim for shore.*
- *Keep the paddle to use as a weapon in case you encounter the culprits who tampered with the canoe.*
- *Take a warm bath, change clothes, and drink some hot tea to recover before you continue your investigation.*

Treat a Poisonous Spider Bite

If you're anywhere in the Western hemisphere, you could encounter a black widow spider, especially if you're outside exploring a woodpile, storage shed, garden, or under rocks. If you're inside, you'll find black widow spiders in dark places like closets or behind furniture. Try to avoid these areas unless you're properly dressed: Wear gloves and long-sleeved shirts and long pants. Shake out your shoes before putting them on. And follow these tips if you find yourself face to face with a black widow.

1 Know how to identify the spider.

The black widow spider's body is about one-half inch long (smaller than a dime), and it has long legs. Look for a shiny black coat with a red-orange or yellow mark in the shape of an hourglass on its stomach.

2 Keep clear.

Black widow spiders are shy but will bite when provoked, trapped, sat upon, or touched.

3 Check for symptoms or characteristic spider-bite marks.

A victim's reaction to the bite varies, depending on where the bite is located, how much venom is injected, and the person's sensitivity to the poison. Some people experience intense pain during the bite or afterward. There's usually little swelling, accompanied by two faint red spots—fang punctures. Eventually the victim will feel pain, such as cramping or rigidity in the abdomen and back. Other symptoms include nausea, sweating, tremors, breathing difficulties, and fever. Symptoms usually disappear after a few days, and the bites rarely cause serious health problems or death, but can make you sick.

4 *Seek medical assistance.*

Apply an ice pack on the bite area to reduce swelling and pain. If possible, find the spider or the parts of the spider, place the specimen in a bag or jar, and bring it along to the hospital for identification.

5 *Administer first aid to the victim.*

- Clean the bite area with soap and water.
- Tie a bandage (not a tourniquet) above the bite to prevent the spread of the venom.
- Apply a cold compress over the bite to slow down the venom, reduce swelling, and relieve pain.
- Keep the affected area elevated to help prevent swelling.
- Offer aspirin or acetaminophen for the pain.
- Apply an antibiotic lotion to protect against infection.

6 *Make sure the victim takes time to recover.*

The victim should remain in the hospital for a day or so. The doctor may administer a specific antivenin to counteract the venom or medication to relieve pain.

Handle a Vicious Dog

She did not move, and the animal grew calmer. Then, as she spoke to him softly, he sniffed her hand. Moments later, Nancy was stroking his thick fur. "Young lady," said Ed Tawley, "I like the way you stood your ground."—The Secret of Shadow Ranch

Nancy often encounters vicious dogs while sleuthing, but she knows how to keep her head and steer clear of an attack. Most dogs are friendly and domesticated, but if you are not familiar with a particular canine, use caution. Even gentle dogs can become aggressive if they are poorly trained, neglected or abused, elderly and cranky, defensive about their litter, or territorial. Here's what you should do if you encounter a vicious dog.

1 Try to prevent an attack.

If confronted by a dog, stand still and allow him to sniff you. Most dogs will leave after determining you're not a threat. Slowly back away when he loses interest.

- Never interfere with a dog that is caring for its puppies.
- Never startle a dog by waking it or throwing an object in its direction.
- Don't disturb a dog while it is eating or drinking.
- Do not run. A dog's instinct will likely be to give chase.
- Do not scream. Speak to the dog in a firm or soothing voice.

❷ *Remain calm if the dog continues to threaten you.*

Pretend you're going to feed the dog by digging into your jacket or handbag. Meanwhile, move the bag between yourself and the dog for protection. Command the dog to lie down in a stern voice. He may obey you automatically. Also try the commands "No!" "Down!" "Sit!" and "Stay!"

- Avoid eye contact with the dog.
- Avoid sudden movements, and don't raise your hand.
- Avoid getting into an argument with the owner. The dog may try to protect him.

❸ *Keep your head if the dog attacks.*

Try to remain upright so the dog can't bite vital organs as easily. Keep your balance with a fight stance—one leg in front of the other.

- Yell for help.
- Try to punch the dog's nose.
- Kick the dog's rib cage to knock the wind out of him.
- Twist or pull the dog's ears, a sensitive spot.
- Protect your throat with your arm, since many dogs lunge for this area.
- If you fall or are knocked to the ground, curl into a ball with your hands over your ears and remain motionless.

❹ *If bitten, seek medical attention immediately.*

Note the type of dog, the vicinity in which you were attacked, and any other details you can provide to the doctor, police, and animal control officials, so the dog can be tested for rabies or removed from the home.

5 *Prevent attacks in the future.*

- Carry pepper spray or an electronic whistle, both inexpensive and excellent safeguards against dog attacks.
- Call the police to alert them of a loose or vicious dog in the area.
- Avoid dogs wandering around the area, especially if the dog is biting randomly at things, looks wild-eyed, or has long strings of saliva dangling from its mouth. He may have rabies.

Tame a Wild Horse— and Keep It from Bucking

When Nancy goes sleuthing at Shadow Ranch, she's as comfortable on a horse as she is investigating a mystery. She's benefited from horseback riding lessons and has lots of experience riding. She's even survived a wild bucking horse ride from time to time. "Horse breaking" or "gentling" is the skill of teaching a horse how to be harnessed and ridden. A horse naturally rejects attempts to ride it, so the process can be challenging.

1 Determine the horse's temperament.

Like people, different horses have different dispositions. Most breeders select their horses for their intelligence, temperament, and trainability. Look for a calm horse that is innately friendly and easily teachable, rather than one that is nervous or excitable.

2 Earn the horse's respect.

Approach the horse and gain his trust by moving slowly and murmuring softly. Most trainers believe in taking a gentle approach toward taming to first gain the trust and cooperation of these large and powerful animals. It's easier to work with a young horse that has already been civilized by an older horse. But if he hasn't, the trainer must respond to

Walk quietly along the left side of the horse
and murmur reassuringly to him.

nips and kicks quickly, with a light cuff on the muzzle or swat on the flank.

3 Choose a method of taming.

Training varies depending on your preference. Some trainers simply throw a saddle on the horse and work to break down his resistance. Some tie the horse to a tree to help him calm down before they begin training. And some mount the horse in water so that he can't struggle too much.

4 Never use anything inhumane to train the horse.

Never use a thin wire or sharp-edged bit, sharpened spurs, extremely forceful restraint systems, or negative reinforcement to train a horse. Those who use these methods just want fast results and don't have the patience to properly train the animal. Instead, use positive reinforcement or behavior modification. Praise and reward your horse when he obeys.

5 Make sure the horse hasn't been tampered with.

If you suspect someone has tampered with your horse—to keep you from pursuing a phantom horse or other clue:

- Walk quietly along the left side of the horse.
- When he whinnies nervously, murmur reassuringly to him and stroke his head.
- Feel the girth to be sure it has not been loosened.
- Check for any nettles that may have been placed under the blanket.
- Run your hand over the bridle to make sure it's in order.

6 Try to keep the horse from bucking.

Grip the pommel tight and hang onto the reins until the horse lands, then wait for someone to hold the horse down so you can fling yourself from the saddle. Bucking can be dangerous for the rider. To rid a horse of this habit:

- Warm up the saddle area. Cover the horse's cold back with a sheepskin numnah or pad.
- Saddle up early. Place the saddle on the horse's back twenty minutes before you ride to give him time to warm up the saddle.
- Check the fit of the saddle. It may be pinching the horse's withers or pressing on the backbone.
- Keep his head up. A horse cannot buck with any force if his head is held high. If he starts to put his head down, pull upward forcefully on the snaffle.
- Give him a little time to expel some of his excess energy after being cooped up for a long period.
- Be prompt with corrections. Tell your horse to stop bucking the second he attempts it, instead of trying to punish him afterward.

7 Know when to get professional help.

When a horse is too much to handle, turn over the reins to a professional trainer. Don't wait too long before seeking assistance, or you may have a wild bucking bronco on your hands.

Escape from Quicksand

*Running ahead of Ned, Nancy paid scant heed to the ground under-
foot, and stepped ankle-deep into a quagmire. When she tried to
retreat, the mud tugged at her feet. . . . "It's quicksand!" Ned cried
hoarsely.*—The Ghost of Blackwood Hall

Quicksand is difficult to get out of, but it doesn't suck
you under as it did in the old *Tarzan* movies. Quicksand
is a concoction of fine sand, clay, and salt water. Since
humans aren't dense enough to sink in it, they float. All
the same, there's nothing like quicksand to trip up even
the most sure-footed amateur gumshoe.

1 Watch where you're going.

Quicksand occurs in swampy areas, near rivers and lakes,
and by the ocean. Keep an eye out for wet, wavy ground,
muddy sinkholes, and marshlike conditions.

2 Try to keep still and fight off the instinct to panic.

Struggling won't make you sink faster, but it doesn't help.
Remember, quicksand is denser than humans, so you can't
really sink. About the deepest you'll go is waist high.

3 Check to see if you're really stuck.

The force you need to escape from quicksand is nearly

equivalent to pulling out a midsize car. The suction can be tremendous, depending on the quicksand's viscosity—the water to sand/mud ratio. Determine whether or not you're really stuck by "swimming" or walking to the edge and attempting to step out. If you can't, you may need assistance to pull you out of the muck and mire.

4 *Stay afloat.*

Think of the quicksand as a pond of thick, muddy water. If you start to panic, take a deep breath, roll your head back, and try to float on your back until help arrives.

5 *Tread water.*

If help doesn't arrive quickly, lift your head up to stop floating, and wiggle your legs. This motion loosens the sandy mixture, allowing you to free your legs.

6 *Find something to grab onto.*

If you can reach a tree limb or root at the edge of the quagmire, grab on and slowly pull yourself out. If you have your handbag, hook the strap onto an outcropping or stump and pull yourself toward it.

7 *Have friends try to pull you out.*

If friends are nearby, tell them to procure a rope. Tie the rope firmly around your waist, while your friends secure the other end around a strong tree to create a pulley counterweight. As they pull the line taut, they'll free you from the muck. (Just don't drag them in along with you.)

Revive a Fainting Victim

Fainting is a common side effect of sleuthing: Nancy and her chums have all fainted at one time or another, as have many of the individuals Nancy has assisted as she goes about solving mysteries. Fainting occurs when blood flow to the brain is temporarily cut off or in short supply. The causes are numerous—stress over a missing heirloom, grief due to a relative's kidnapping, anxiety, overheating, dehydration, exhaustion, or illness. It's usually temporary, and the victim can be revived in a few minutes. Here are some ways to recognize and treat a fainting spell.

1 Watch for signs of swooning.

If a person says she feels lightheaded, dizzy, or begins to sway or swoon, she may be about to faint. If she complains of blurred vision, sudden perspiration, or waves of nausea, these are also signs of a fainting spell. If she looks pale, is cool to the touch, or flushes suddenly, she may be headed for the floor.

2 Try to catch the person before she hits the ground.

As soon as you suspect a person is fainting, have her sit down and put her head between her legs. If necessary, catch her so she doesn't hit her head on the floor or cause herself other injuries. Once you've got her in your arms, lay her down gently.

Emergency Measures

If the person you are attempting to revive is unresponsive or does not regain consciousness quickly, and you suspect a more serious condition, call for emergency medical assistance. While waiting for help to arrive:

- Check to see if there is some obstruction in her throat or airway and clear it using the Heimlich maneuver.
- Tip her head back to clear her airway.
- If the victim has ceased breathing, administer mouth-to-mouth resuscitation.
- If you cannot detect a heartbeat, begin cardiopulmonary resuscitation.
- If the victim is breathing and a heartbeat is detectable, lay the victim on her back and elevate her legs to help the flow of blood to the brain.
- Apply a cool, damp cloth to her forehead.
- Loosen tight clothing, especially at the neck and waist, so she can breathe more easily.

3 Make sure it's not something other than a fainting spell.

Fainting may mask something serious, such as low blood sugar in a diabetic, a heart attack, a stroke, or internal bleeding. Fainting is not the same as being unconscious. A person who is unconscious won't respond to your attempts to revive her. (See "Emergency Measures," above.)

4 Keep the victim prone.

A fainting spell usually lasts only a minute or two before the victim awakens. During this time the body increases the amount of blood reaching the brain, which remedies itself quickly. It's important to keep the victim lying down to allow this to happen.

5 Handle the victim with care.

Administering spirits of ammonia and smelling salts to fainting victims has fallen out of fashion since they're unpleasant, uncommon, and unnecessary. Don't do anything to the victim that may cause more harm, such as slap her, shake her, throw water on her, move her unnecessarily, or force her stand or sit up. Simply help keep her still and comfortable. Apply a cool washcloth to her forehead. Do not leave her unattended.

6 Slowly let the victim sit up.

Allow the victim to rest in a prone position for some time after she's revived. When she's ready to rise, help her up slowly to allow the body to adjust and improve the flow of oxygen to the brain.

Note Pretending to faint is a great way to fool criminals and escape a possible attack.

Nancy's First-Aid Essentials

Each time she has taken a case, Nancy invariably has had to rescue a victim in need of basic medical assistance. Here's a rundown of some of the quick first-aid techniques she has administered during her lengthy sleuthing career.

- **When a victim falls unconscious in a dust storm.**

  Always carry a handkerchief. You can lay it gently over the victim's face to prevent inhalation of dust particles.

- **When a victim has a swollen ankle.**

  This may be due to a spider bite or sprain, so examine the area first. Then bathe the ankle in cool water, dry it off, and bind it with a bandage that's been treated with an antiseptic.

- **When a victim has fallen into a creek or lake.**

  Make sure she's breathing normally and there's no water in her nose or mouth. If there is, begin mouth-to-mouth resuscitation and CPR.

- **When a victim has a cut on an arm or leg.**

  Get out a clean handkerchief and tie it around the wound to stop the bleeding and protect it.

- **When a victim has a cut on a finger.**

  If the cut is on the victim's finger, place the finger in ice water. Retrieve a bottle of witch hazel, and soak a cotton ball in the liquid. Apply it to the cut, and secure it with a bandage.

- **In case of fire.**

  If you find yourself trapped in a burning building filled with thick smoke, go to the powder room and hold a towel under the faucet. When it's wet, ring it out, then tie it over your nose and mouth to protect yourself from breathing the toxic smoke.

- **The best remedy for just about everything.**

  A cup of hot tea will cure most any disease, injury, or condition.

Keep Your Head and Persist Against All Odds

Nancy went to the front door, opened it, and walked outside. She breathed deeply of the lovely morning air and headed for the rose garden. She let the full beauty of the estate sink into her consciousness, before permitting herself to think further about the knotty problem before her. —The Hidden Staircase

How does Nancy Drew keep her head, stay calm, and avoid panic under the most stressful conditions? She's faced kidnappers, thieves, mobsters, thugs, and vicious beasts without breaking much of a sweat. Much of what she's learned has come from her father, Carson Drew, who advises her on how to remain steady and clear-headed under stressful conditions. Here are tips to help you keep your cool.

1 Clear your mind.

Try not to think of the downside of your situation. Take several deep breaths; try to relax your body and unclutter your mind.

2 Brainstorm possible solutions.

Toss out all possibilities, then narrow them down to the ones that are most practical. Put them in order of possible success, then begin to imagine the outcome of each.

3 *Be realistic about the solutions.*

When you've weeded out the least valid options, be realistic about the remaining solutions before you proceed.

4 *Believe in your ability to solve your problem.*

If you think positively and believe in your innate strengths and abilities, you're more likely to come up with a solution. Don't think about all the things that can go wrong or you'll just make things worse.

5 *Use your brain, not your emotions.*

Feelings can cloud your thoughts, so try to keep them at bay. When you use your cognitive skills instead of your emotions, you're more likely to find a solution that works.

6 *Take a break.*

Try a change of scenery when tackling a problem. The different surroundings may help you brainstorm fresh ideas and see things with a fresh perspective.

7 *Keep your spirits up.*

Give yourself positive affirmations. Drink herbal tea or eat hot soup to relax. Take a drive through the country or a walk through the park. Call a friend and chat. Take a warm bath. Eat some chocolate. Listen to music. Refresh yourself with a pep talk and a treat, and you'll be ready to face the challenge.

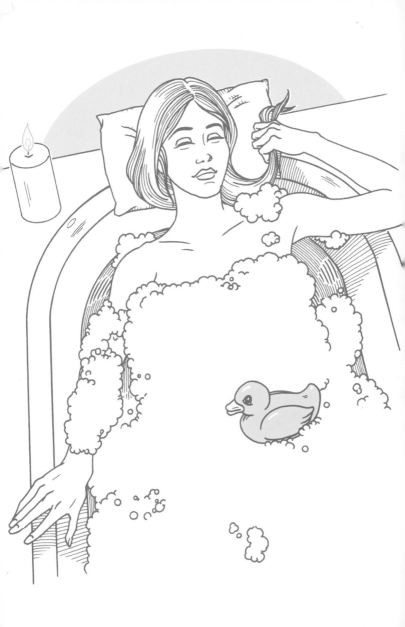